I Looked for God's Absence: FRANCE

I LOOKED FOR GOD'S ABSENCE:

France

Irenaeus Rosier, o.carm.

SHEED AND WARD - NEW YORK

© SHEED & WARD, INC., 1960

LIBRARY OF CONGRESS CATALOG CARD NUMBER: 60-12877

Cum licentia superiorum

NIHIL OBSTAT:

    THOMAS J. MCHUGH, LL.D.

    Censor Librorum

APRIL 29, 1960

IMPRIMATUR:

    ✠ JEROME D. HANNAN

    Bishop of Scranton

MAY 16, 1960

TRANSLATED FROM THE DUTCH BY ILONA RICARDO

MANUFACTURED IN THE UNITED STATES OF AMERICA

Preface

IT WAS not my intention to publish the diary entries I made of my findings about the religious and moral values hidden beneath the appearance of dechristianization among the workers of France. I might never have got around to writing down my experiences if I hadn't been emphatically asked to do so from various sides. A scholarly publication was all I had in mind for the result of my studies. When I here describe actual situations and encounters as well as personal impressions of regions, I do not do so only because of those many requests, but also because the problems and sufferings of the people I came to know have become identified with my own existence to such an extent that I want to express them for anyone who takes to heart the condition of his fellow-men.

The material for these notes was gathered in the mines of France, where I worked from July 1951 to February 1952. Because of the nature of this account, no one should expect to find in it a scientific synthesis. The material itself will, I hope, give food for thought. Here and there I give my personal reflections, for the nature of my studies would not allow me to register impressions altogether objectively, but involved me in situations and opinions I had to straighten out in my own mind. Likewise, I could not distort reality by leaving out what might seem indelicate and coarse to some.

The notes published here represent a heterogeneous mass of data with which I wanted to explain every-day religious, moral and social life in France. This is not a collection of interviews on a specific theme, but a mixture of events, situations, personal thoughts, and reactions. It might be noted here that it is impossible to write down every conversation, observation and occurrence. It should be clear from the outset that during my six-month stay among the French workers, I got to know more people than I describe here. I only wanted to illustrate what is alive among the people though it may not be immediately apparent. This book has become a description of situations and cases which can be taken objectively as symptomatic of a whole class, and not only as isolated events. Taken subjectively, it is the product of a great many impressions. I have simply tried to give a picture of the workers' world in France as I experienced it when I was part of it.

Because these notes were not put down with publication in mind, I wrote without any preconceptions. This is, after all, the only way to be as unbiased as possible. Where necessary I have made people and places anonymous or pseudonymous.

I Looked for God's Absence: FRANCE

1

THE cloudless blue sky of Rome promised us a hot day when we arrived at Termini station early on the morning of the 2nd of July, 1951. The station was already crowded, despite the early hour, as is always the case when important trains are about to leave. We were surrounded by nervous bustling, casual indifference, shouting, shoving, pent-up silence—according to the character and destinations of the travelers.

A train full of people, for the most part unknown to one another, started to move. The baggage racks were scanned for space by incoming compartment-sharing travelers, each with two, three or four heavily laden suitcases; decisive, hesitant, timid, self-assured, melancholy, friendly—all kinds of people.

Young fellows ran alongside the moving train for a short way, as if at the very last moment they still had something important to say to a head poked through a window. Women dabbed their eyes with handkerchiefs. People waved and nodded; one could see every variety of emotion passing our window like a movie. A mysterious world, that world of human beings, with its meetings and partings, its bonds and its distances, its sorrow, guilt, joy, love, comedy—its perpetually fresh experience of the commonplace.

In the corridor people went on pushing and shoving until finally all had found places. Like a sower with seed-filled hands the train was to broadcast us left and right, all over Europe. There would be new encounters, fresh joy and sorrow.

I was on my way to France. What would await me at the end
of my journey I knew only vaguely. I was to work as a common
laborer so that the workers' world might speak to me in its own
language; to be part of the community of those whose lives I had
known until now only as an outsider and an observer, to share
their experience of the same milieu and background, to share in
the fatigue of their work and undergo the same hardships. Of
course I had been meeting and talking with workers since I was
quite young. I had good friends among them, and I had not been
brought up in luxury myself. There wasn't really any significant
distance between my background and theirs. But they had been
more or less prosperous workers, such as one meets in the smaller
towns in Holland, and their world was by no means that of the
bigger industries. As an adult I had become acquainted with
workers' problems through literature, I had visited many big industries, I had gone down into the mines and become familiar
with the housing in the large workers' colonies. I had already
talked with many workers in that world, as well as with others
having much to do with them either because of their position in
the industry or through their studies. One might think this enough
to know about existing conditions. But I had never been convinced of it. All real knowledge of life comes from participation.
I had no criteria—at least no satisfying criteria—for estimat-
ing the value of all that had been said and written. What I
needed was to work alongside the workers, establishing with
them another tie than the one deriving from our common human
destiny.

I was aware that this kind of effort to get to know the workers'
world from the inside might meet with criticism and skepticism.
It might be considered a dilettante's curiosity which could never
develop into a full participation in the life of the workers—on the
one hand because my education differed totally from theirs; on
the other because I would always be able to withdraw from their

hardships. I even knew in advance that I could not be among them in France for more than six months, since other activities awaited me after that. Because of all this I was running the risk of getting an illusory experience of a romantic sort, which I might use in an arrogant way for my own purposes, and thus become a cause of irritation among the workers as well as to outsiders. This would have been all the more true if it were not for the experiences I have mentioned which preceded the undertaking. It might even hold true if I were not to continue my connection with the world I would come to know in this way. However, I can testify that if any element of romanticism or dilettantism had been in my attitude at the outset, it disappeared completely after the first week.

It was not only the motive of sociological research that impelled me to share the lives of these people in their various phases. For myself, the scientific urge was not even the strongest one. I love life and I love people, and it is my right to join with them so long as higher obligations don't prevent me. The experience of these worlds is worth more to me than whatever scientific results may come with it. It is part of the experience of my existence as a human being, the encounter with those who share this earthly pilgrimage of mine; the encounter, too, with God in them.

Because I cannot and would not present my experiences otherwise than as an effort to acquaint myself with the problems of the workers' world as closely as possible, I want to tell here simply what happened to me and the conclusions I drew from these events. What follows is not in the area of a scientific discourse; it consists of edited diary entries of a diversified nature. Insofar as I draw any conclusions, they are my own, and anyone is free to disagree with me when his arguments are stronger than mine. It may not be possible for one single human being to grasp the problems of an entire class of people from his own experiences. The observations and criticism of others are even necessary if we are to give objective reality the respect we owe it.

2

My journey took me first, by way of Marseilles, to Aix-en-Provence to meet a certain Father Thomas. I had been told that he knew the religious situation in France well from experience, and that it would be important for me to talk to him before choosing my exact field of endeavor. It was late in the evening when I arrived. I was received cordially in spite of the fact that my host was busy preparing to leave the next day for Arbresle, near Lyons. By a happy coincidence I had to go next to the same place, so we should meet again. That evening, however, there wasn't much time to go into serious discussion.

He was the embodiment of French charm and was courteous to me in every respect. Yet I suspected that he had a certain skepticism regarding my plans. There had been dilettante adventurers of unpleasant memory who had sought contact with the workers' world for a time and afterwards considered themselves experts. And among the priests who had devoted considerable time to living among the workers there had been several who lost their faith.

What did I hope to achieve in a foreign country among workers whose dialect I might scarcely understand? Wasn't it clear in advance that my enterprise would come to nothing? What if I were to make mistakes? Should I take that risk, in view of the fact that worker-priests had been discredited in many circles? Wouldn't that make the situation worse?

He didn't say all this to my face, but I understood it as the meaning behind some of his friendly remarks.

What were my credentials in face of those objections?

I would not preach the faith among the workers as a worker-priest. Neither did I intend to gather statistics on my own, based on questionnaires or formal interviews. There were already enough statistics to provide a fair idea of the religious situation in France. But the criteria in this kind of investigation had always been more or less those of the formal Church: the number baptized, the number practising, the number who received the last rites and the number buried with church ritual. These figures raise the question: is there any religious conviction left among the non-practising, and if so, what does it consist of? One should also ask oneself what the actual belief of the practising is. My intention was only to probe these matters in the framework of the spontaneous, informal contacts of a friend among friends. Very little research of that kind had been done by competent people. But it would be arrogance on my part to consider myself competent, and anyone is entitled to doubt it if the results of my study do not convince him. In this respect, Father Thomas's reserve was the justifiable attitude of a wise and cautious man.

My study would certainly not produce statistics. It would be entirely qualitative in nature as against the quantitative character of the statistical studies. Had there ever been a key to interpret the statistics? Weren't existing interpretations often based on assumptions that, though founded on experience in some cases, were too subjective and uninformed? Is membership in political parties sufficient basis for judging people's inner attitude toward life? When people answer a questionnaire by stating that they are non-believers or atheists, what does this mean in reality? How can a clergy that has no contact with the non-practising laity judge what goes on inside them?

Father Thomas arranged for me to stay with the Petites Soeurs de Charles de Foucauld, where I would also be able to celebrate Mass the next morning. I had never heard of their existence and was happily surprised by the genuine Christian hospitality with

which they received me. It was a young community. I had the
impression that none of the members were over thirty years old.
There weren't any conventual formalities. I joined them in their
recreation period, while they quenched my thirst with a pitcher
of delicious green mint water. The atmosphere was as fresh as a
spiritual spring.

The Little Sisters are clothed like poor women, in pale blue
dresses, and they lead a life of real poverty in quarters devoid of
comforts and conveniences. There are communities of men of the
same order. These men and women, contemplative and active in
their way of life, are an example of the ever-renewed freshness of
Christ's gospel as they put Christian love and brotherhood into
practice in a materialistic and secularized society.

The chapel where I said Mass the next day was a large room
with a starkly plain altar, and I was given vestments to wear
which were magnificent in their simplicity. The only seats were
low stools, placed in a semi-circle. The sisters knelt on the floor
as they said their office together and made their long meditations.
Contemplatives in the midst of life!

It has become a general opinion among Christians that France
is in a bad state. It is supposed to be a Catholic country, but the
prevailing opinion is that Catholicism is hard to find there today.

However that may be, one still finds in France a faith that can
move mountains and is touching in the heroic love with which the
Gospel is put into practice. Among the communities in which the
spirit of the Gospel is most forcefully expressed is that of the
followers of Charles de Foucauld. The order for men is called
"Les petits Frères de Jésus," "en souvenir de Sa récommendation
tant répétée d'être petits et de Son conseil de nous appeler frères."

They live from day to day on their workers' wages. "They are
not allowed to have personal property but must live from the
labor of their hands in great poverty like our Lord Jesus."

They live the life of the poor as to lodgings and dress. When
they are sick, they share the lot of the poor as to hospital and
social care. The poor man's fatigue and insecurity in day-to-day
living are for them a way to inner self-searching. They make the

three vows of poverty, chastity and obedience. Among their comrades in need they are to be in all milieus *"comme les permanents de la prière."*

They spend an hour daily in adoration before the Blessed Sacrament. The spirit of continuous prayer must penetrate their daily work, their fellowship and all other aspects of their lives. They are not intent on achieving great things but must remain modest and humble—friends and brothers to all. In small groups they go where the Church sends them. By preference they go to the abandoned and live among those who are rejected or despised by the world.

They are to be found among the agricultural and industrial workers of France, in the mines, among hospital personnel, among the Arab nomads of the desert and the proletariat of the city. They can be found among the fishermen of Brittany and the lepers of Africa, and sometimes even among those without hope, such as the displaced persons who have no homeland.

The poor should feel at home with them, since they share bed and board with those who have no roof over their heads, with the unemployed, and with vagabonds. All this to establish unity and brotherhood in love. There are priests and laymen among them with no distinction in their way of living. Their novitiate is in the Arabian desert. They have been in existence since 1933.

Because of the heavy luggage I had left at the station I did not accompany Father Thomas on the bus to Avignon but went by train via Marseilles. We met again in Lyons and went together to Arbresle.

In Arbresle a big villa, almost a small castle, stands in the midst of the woods, in the ideal quiet of unspoiled nature. It is now a Dominican monastery, a center for Economy and Humanism, an organization of scientists who study the social problems of France. At the head of it is Father Lebret, O. P. He had invited me to visit him before beginning my studies in France.

I was lucky, for a scientific congress was about to begin, and among the participants I would meet people who could give me valuable information and help. From all parts of France they came to bring the results of their social investigations. There were also interested outsiders from abroad—the United States, Canada, Uruguay, Italy—and I found myself suddenly representing Holland.

The meeting rooms were rather bare and poorly equipped, and much had to be improvised to accommodate about fifty people, but the atmosphere was pleasant and amicable.

Father Lebret is an elderly priest who is a serious man of science. "For years," he said, "I have been toying with the problem that you want to study, but it has always remained extremely difficult for me to describe what the religion of the people really is. You will find out for yourself that the French don't give of themselves very easily. But I am very curious. Keep me informed of your findings. Since you have had some experience in Germany, it would perhaps be best for you to start in Alsace-Lorraine. After that you should work in the North, and perhaps also in Paris for a while. Among the participants in the congress you will find people who can help you find the work you want."

The lectures gave me some idea of the social conditions in the French cities and the countryside. But they were based on quantitative statistics, and only a few of them touched on the theme which was absorbing me. The contact I had with the participants between the lectures was more important. The walks together through the woods surrounding the buildings were a delight.

Father Egidius, professor at the Institut Catholique in Paris and one of the guests in Arbresle, agreed with me that the statistical studies on the religious situation in France and other countries needed to be supplemented by qualitative research. He had started it himself, but what he meant by qualitative research boiled down to a more intensive study of a smaller territory; for instance, a detailed analysis of a parish community with reference to the probable causes of existing conditions. It seemed to me, however, that this way of working did not essentially differ from the ordinary statistical methods, and should be called a genetic rather than a qualitative study.

The answer to the question of what religion means to people is not provided by statistics, no matter how detailed. Father Egidius had not applied the non-directive interview, which I considered the only method for this kind of study. To me this method seems indispensable if one wants to find out what people's attitude toward life is.

There is an existentialist basis for the religious feeling, which man either shows on the outside or represses because of certain circumstances. I told Father Egidius how I would sometimes, during the course of a conversation, give an analysis of human existence and its inclination towards transcendence, and how I had found that my listeners became more than normally interested and would agree with my views.

As a sequel to such an analysis one might show the function in human life of Revelation, of Grace and of the Church, since life's highest fulfillment lies in those three things.

The existentialist religious feeling is present even under the appearance of indifference, where there seems to be no religion and even antagonism towards it. In apostolic activity one should start from there. But usually we look for psychological and social causes to explain religious decay and concentrate on the removal of those obstacles, overlooking this deep-rooted sense of religion. (That is my objection to the otherwise excellent book by Simon Ligier, *Psychologie Pastorale*, which had just appeared.)

These views as to an analysis of human existence as the starting point for apostolic activity got response from others also. Professor Gauthier insisted that I should stop at the Major Seminary in Dijon to have further discussions with his colleagues. I would have liked to do this but didn't find the time. The fact that it was possible for me to alternate six months of teaching with six months of actual work in community life was, everyone felt, a fortunate situation.

My stay in Arbresle was extremely useful because of the people I met there. We lived a communal life; we set and cleared the table ourselves and sang grace in French before and after meals. Everyone gave a talk about his activities during the past year. I had to join in, mobilizing all my French to inform my audience at some length about my work—no slight matter, for I had had very little practice in conversational French.

Among those present was the Abbé L., spiritual adviser to the engineers in northern France. He was prepared to help me find work when I came north.

"The way you are going about it is the only way to get to know people," he said. "I myself worked incognito as a laborer for several months. When I finally told them I was a priest, the nature of my contact with my co-workers changed immediately. From that time they didn't talk in my presence about many things I had previously shared with them as a matter of course."

Mme. Gérard Nilence, one of the participants in the congress, was to drive me in her car from Arbresle to Alsace-Lorraine on July 16th. She thought she might find me a job in the iron mines with the help of a brother-in-law, Edouard Nilence. He was the engineer for a group of iron mines, and in charge of modernizing them. He was married to the daughter of the chief administrator of another group of mines. But for the time being I rejected his help; an ordinary worker wouldn't have it!

I went to the employment bureau in the nearby town, but I was told that very few foreign workers were being hired. There was no need for labor in the big industries, only in the mines and in agriculture, but then I would have to sign a contract. What should I do next? A contract would tie me down to a specific mine for at least a year, and I had to keep the necessary freedom of movement to get to know the workers' milieus in different industries.

I was aware that this very factor distinguished me from an ordinary worker. But I hoped the difference would not prevent me from sharing the essence of their lives.

I had no choice but to confess that I couldn't be tied to a con-

tract and that I wanted to work in order to get acquainted with
the problems of the different industries.

"Then you will have to work as an apprentice."

"Will I?"

"Do you know how to go about it?"

"No!"

"You ask the Dutch government to introduce you as an apprentice to the French government. If the French government agrees,
you will be able to get a salary as an official apprentice, but in
exchange the Dutch government will have to allow a French
apprentice to work in Holland at their expense."

I consulted friends in The Hague who had offered help in case
of need. They made inquiries at the ministries concerned, but
soon concluded that it would take too long to get the necessary
papers and that, if possible, I should find other means.

In the meantime I had done so. The chief administrator of the
iron mines had been informed of my desire to work and live as a
common laborer in order to acquaint myself with the spiritual
problems of the workers' world. He was greatly interested. He
sent me a message to go to the biggest iron mine under his jurisdiction, which was in the village of Filondange; the director had
been told I was coming.

3

ONE warm afternoon I put on my blue overalls, put some indispensable articles in my knapsack and took the bus in the direction
of Luxembourg. When I reached my bus stop I found that the
mine was about five miles beyond it, and there was no immediate

connection. I would have to wait an hour and a half. I decided
to walk, for I wanted to get there before the director's office
closed.

I soon began to feel the heat, and the walk seemed endless. At
last, from a slope, I saw before me the village of Filondange and
what I thought must be the mine, far away in the valley on my
left. A picturesque sight, the village—white houses with red roofs
in the midst of trees, and a church against a hill in the background. It didn't give an impression of poverty. I walked into the
village. But these weren't laborers' cottages. Pleasant, comfort-
able-looking houses with little front yards, well kept in the style
of a prosperous middle class. And I saw hardly any men that
could pass for workers.

I asked where the mine was.

"The mine itself or the colony, the workers' houses?"

"The mine itself."

"First street to the left."

So the workers' colony was apart from the village. Besides, "the
first street on the left" made any further directions superfluous.
It ran on through the colony. Sidewalks disappeared. The two-
story houses became a dirty gray, monotonously identical, badly
in need of paint, with here and there a door open or a woman
leaning out of a window. It was quite a different story from the
village of Filondange.

I passed some barracks, built exactly like the other houses. Two
sturdy young fellows were sitting on a window sill. Either one of
these giants could have sent me reeling with a box on the ear.
They were shouting to some friends inside. They sounded as if
they knew it all—no one could tell them anything! The thought
came to me that it would be rough going inside there, and I had
a secret hope that there would be other barracks.

It was another two miles to the mine. I saw blocks of houses
and more blocks of houses, all the same. Here and there workers
were sitting on the roadside staring straight ahead of them. I
nodded and mumbled something in passing, but they didn't
respond.

Tired and perspiring, I arrived at the director's office. All the windows of the clerks' cubicles were closed. I knocked at one of them, and someone opened it. Could I speak with the director? The man looked at me with surprise. Probably a strange question at an unusual hour.

"The director is busy, what do you want?" A painful situation.

"He is expecting me."

"Your name?" I told him. He left, returned and opened a door for me.

"Come right in." He went ahead of me, knocked at the private office, opened the door and showed me in.

I faced a man of about forty, serious and somewhat withdrawn. He stood up behind his desk and shook hands with me.

"Please sit down. You want to work in the mine here?" All this in a grave, matter-of-fact tone.

"If possible, yes!"

Although there was no reason for it, I felt ill at ease, as if I had been reprimanded or was about to take an exam.

"Probably you want to go underground, where most of the workers are."

"I'd like to."

"You think you're strong enough for this kind of work?"

"I hope so." He frowned. He seemed to consider it a risky undertaking.

"I can hardly let you go without a medical examination first."

"I don't object to that."

"Well, if that's the case . . . ." He looked at me thoughtfully. "Your spectacles are really a serious drawback, but I'm willing to make an exception. There are others who wear glasses."

"Thank you."

"How long do you plan to stay here?"

"If possible, at least a month."

"We don't usually take workers for only a month. If you really want to get to know the workers, you'll have to work above ground, too. They are quite a different kind of people."

"I've no objection."

"You'll have to be satisfied with the lowest grade of work, like all new men. If I gave you something more important to do, it would cause discontent."

"But I wouldn't want anything else."

"I'll give you an ordinary worker's wages."

"Thank you."

"And now, where do you plan to live?"

"With the workers."

He smiled for the first time.

"So you won't accept an invitation to be my guest?"

"You will understand, I hope, that I can hardly do that if I want to know every aspect of the life of the workers."

He grew serious again.

"Yet I would appreciate it if you would come to see me from time to time to tell me your impressions."

"I hope you'll excuse me, but I'd rather have no contact with you or any other officials during the time I work here."

"You think the workers are that much against us?"

"I don't know!"

"But anyone who has complaints or difficulties can always come to me!"

"Yes, but still . . . ."

"In any case I hope to see you before you leave."

"That goes without saying."

"If you want to be one of the workers, you'll have to live in the barracks."

"That's what I want."

"You won't find it as easy as all that. But anyway, there's nowhere else to live."

He now became very cordial.

"Do you need money, by any chance, or anything else?"

"I think I can get by until I get paid."

"Well, if you should find yourself in difficulty, come to me. I live over there." He pointed through the window to a villa and wrote his name on a slip of paper, which he handed me.

"And now I'll introduce you to Monsieur Piron, the chief of personnel. He is a good Catholic, his son is studying for the priesthood. He is the only one except myself who knows you are a priest. I also want to tell you that you'll be classified officially as an apprentice, otherwise you'd have to sign a contract. And another thing, you will have to state in writing that in case of accident, you will take full responsibility. Monsieur Piron will let you know about the medical examination. He'll tell you in which barracks you can live and give you your registration papers."

He made a phone call, and M. Piron shortly appeared—a war invalid. He got his instructions and we left.

Apparently M. Piron thought the case very important and impressive. As the father of a seminarian he talked to me like a sort of brother-in-arms. I must not fail to visit him one evening. I had done right by coming to Filondange. There wasn't any Catholic activity among the workers and never, to his knowledge, had a priest worked in this way in the entire mine complex.

"But you must understand that I'm not going to do any pastoral work here!"

Yes, he knew, but still it was important for me to be there.

He wrote a note for barracks no. 2 and a few lines to the doctor.

"Do you know where your barracks is?"

"No."

He told me how to get there, and it became clear to me that it was the very barracks I had just passed. Well, I had started something and would have to go all the way.

"Could I help you with an old bicycle by any chance? I've got one that I don't use any more. It's nothing special, but it's still usable."

It wasn't a bad idea, for the barracks were more than a mile and a half from the mine.

"Go to the doctor tomorrow morning at eight o'clock, and see me at my office after that. Then I'll give you the things you need

and assign you to a group. You can take the bicycle at the same
time."

We shook hands warmly. "See you tomorrow."

I found myself in the street again. In front of me lay the mine,
an unsightly complex of dirty buildings. There was a shunting of
trains and I saw dump-carts loaded with brown pieces of ore
coming out of a tunnel. All of it was still a closed world to me,
harsh and formless.

The entrance to the barracks was as small as those of the
surrounding houses. I went up some steps, came into a small hall
and saw that two folding doors led into a kind of dining hall, a
room with big unpainted tables and a number of benches and
stools. At one of the windows a few young men were sitting. I
went to the counter and handed over an envelope addressed to
the boss. I was told he wasn't there at the moment, and would I
please wait a few minutes. The envelope was handed back to me.
I waited fifteen minutes, inquired again; he wasn't back yet. Half
an hour, three quarters of an hour, an hour. I sat there not knowing what to do. Now and then someone came in without uttering
a sound and left again.

Finally the man I wanted appeared behind the counter.

"Yes?"

I gave him the letter. He opened it, rubbed his bald head and
shrugged his shoulders hopelessly.

"You're supposed to be billeted here?"

"Yes."

"Damn it, they know there's no room here. Impossible."

"Well . . . where am I to go?"

He made an angry gesture. "The only thing for me to do is
pack up and leave. What a mess!"

For a while he said nothing. Then: "There's only one thing to
do, you'll have to share a room with my son. I'll put you up
somewhere else later."

He left without another word, and I was alone again. I put my
things in a corner and waited. The room gradually filled up with

clumsy, shouting men. It was time for dinner. I hung back against the wall and watched. Nobody took any notice of me.

An aluminum bowl with macaroni soup was put on one of the tables and a tray with spoons and forks next to it. The men took plates from a pile on the counter and helped themselves to soup. After that they found themselves seats, maneuvering with plates in hand. After watching for a few minutes I made my way through the crowd and did the same. Most of the men took little notice of one another, each seemed to go his own way. Opposite me sat a boy who recognized me as a newcomer and gave me a friendly nod, but didn't say anything. I hadn't yet got my bearings enough to join in the conversations, and I kept a little apart. I wasn't the only one.

The men lined up in front of the counter with the plates from which they'd eaten their soup. I joined them and received in my turn a piece of meat, some potatoes and salad. The boss, who was serving, smiled at me. Apparently he had cooled off. He handed me a large loaf of bread. The others had received theirs at an earlier meal. I was given to understand that it had to last me a day. If you paid extra, you could get a glass of wine or beer. I asked for beer, but I didn't have to pay. That would be taken care of later, probably because I hadn't yet been paid.

The food wasn't bad, but everyone was complaining that it was the same old thing again.

When I had my portion and was about to go back to my seat, I saw that it had been taken. I had to find somewhere else to sit. Meanwhile the tables had become soiled with spilled soup, pieces of bread and other food. A few dogs went around sniffing and trying to gobble up leavings. Nobody said a prayer; it was a chaotic meal from beginning to end. The more so because people kept coming and going. Each group had about an hour for eating. An hour later the same thing would start all over again for those coming from the afternoon shift. It was all rather rough-and-ready. One thing I did notice, however, was that several husky fellows were wearing chains with crosses or medallions around their necks.

I slept in a part of the barracks that was reserved for the boss and his family and which could be reached only by a separate staircase. Downstairs a big St. Bernard stood guard, and on the second floor a harmless hunting dog, but on the third floor, where I slept under the roof, there was another hunting dog that barked wildly when I went up the stairs and bit me in the leg the very first evening. The next evening he took a piece out of my trouser leg. After that I was transferred to another dormitory.

I had to go to the doctor at 8 A.M. There were at least ten people ahead of me when I arrived. I sat down next to a young African and tried to copy his patience.

A young man in a white coat kept opening the door and calling for the next patient. I took him to be an assistant, but it turned out that he was the doctor himself. He read my note and looked at me in surprise.

"You must be an apprentice?"

It was my turn to look surprised, for it wasn't mentioned in the note.

"Yes."

"You're not French?"

"No, Dutch."

"Are you going to stay here long?"

"About a month."

"For what purpose do you work on probation?"

"It's my intention to work for various industries and get to know the workers' problems first-hand."

Meanwhile he was tapping my chest. "You smoke a lot?"

"Yes."

"You will have trouble with your glasses. I hope it won't be too awkward."

He was very friendly. "Where do you live?"

"In the barracks."

"In the barracks?"

"Yes, where else?"

"You are studying a very important subject and using a very thorough method. I know a priest in Larache who is doing the same thing. He is a psychologist, but he works entirely incognito. He is a friend of mine."

I looked at him in surprise but didn't say anything. It might be worthwhile to get in touch with that priest. What were his exact intentions and methods? (Unfortunately I never succeeded in establishing contact with him. When I wanted to ask his address three weeks later, the doctor was on vacation. Even the clergy in the neighborhood didn't seem to know of his existence.)

The doctor gave me a written note to the effect that I had passed the examination, and I left.

As arranged, I met M. Piron at the mine. The thought that I would be treated as an ordinary laborer had apparently been too much for him. He had informed several departments which were to give me my tools that I was an apprentice. He had not exactly rendered me a service by that, but it now was too late to do anything about it. The inevitable result was that I got more consideration: an electric lamp instead of a carbide lamp, a locker for my clothes with the foremen, whose shower I could use too. Why was I living in the barracks and not in what was called the casino, a building with more comforts and better service, where the apprentices usually lived?

The chief engineer suggested a visit to the different sections of the mine to see the interesting technical operations, and was surprised when I told him that I appreciated his proposal but preferred getting to know the mine by working in it. He was to cause me a lot of trouble later, precisely because he meant so well. He tried continually to treat me with special respect—this because I was a Dutchman. Fortunately the workers didn't seem to notice much. Besides, in their eyes an apprentice is only one of themselves. Apprentices usually come from workers' families and are sent to a mining school so that later they can become foremen. The foremen who don't come from a mining school are recruited from among workers with special qualifications. So if

the workers considered me an apprentice, this did not necessarily
create a barrier between us. They do have a naive admiration
and respect for anything that has to do with knowledge and
education. But the fact that I lived with them was enough to
make me belong, and soon I took part in all their activities.

The barracks where I lived had been constructed with as little
regard for appearance as had the surrounding workers' cottages.
The style—or rather the lack of it—was identical. About 50 un-
married workers lived in it, and about 200, who lived in the
nearby houses, came in for their meals. So one would expect it
to be a building designed for 50 sleepers and 250 eaters, but in
reality it differed from the other houses only in that it was slightly
longer.

Narrow stone steps with a railing led to the door. If three boys
were standing on the top step, nobody could get in or out. The
entrance was no wider than that of an ordinary house, so that it
was always jammed at rush hours. Right behind the door, which
was usually open, was a small hallway leading to a spiral staircase; the kitchen door and the folding doors to the dining room
opened off it. The interior of the house was as gray and dull as
the exterior.

I have already described the procedure at mealtimes. Soon I
found that the same menu was served almost every day. And
many of the men complained about the quantity, too. I must say,
however, that I was always satisfied with my portion. They also
griped about the quality. Griping seemed to fill a deep need.

The dining room was the only room in the house that could
have served as a gathering place outside mealtimes. But nobody
ever made use of it. There wasn't a single diversion: no living
room, no reading room, no radio—nothing that afforded even a
minimum of comfort.

During the day the outside wall of the house was lined with
bicycles. Almost everybody had one, for the mine, as I have said,
was quite a distance off. But there was no garage or anywhere
else to put them. The only thing you could do was drag your

bicycle up the narrow, winding staircase at night to the upstairs hall. But there wasn't room enough even there for all of them. The hall was no wider than would let two or three men pass each other at most, and it was dark, receiving only indirect light from the transoms over doors of the rooms. But even the transoms were partly blacked out by the trousers and other clothing hung behind them. It took all your concentration to avoid breaking your neck over the bicycles already there, and usually you had to keep your bicycle beside your bed.

Each room was shared by four men. Almost the entire floor space was taken up by the beds and chests—the latter just large enough to receive the most necessary clothing. (The rest had to be kept in suitcases on top of the chests.) There were no tables or chairs. If anyone wanted to write a letter, he had to do it across his knees or go to the dining room—but nobody would think of taking the latter course. The linen was changed once every two or three weeks, and it was always streaked with brown from the iron ore.

I slept in a room with three roommates, all between twenty and thirty. None of them was completely healthy. Two were obviously victims of advanced silicosis, a disease caused by the accumulation of dust in the lungs. In spite of the summer weather they couldn't bear to sleep with the windows open; they slept badly and coughed almost continuously. They usually woke up groaning with a headache, and cursing. *"Quelle vie!"* What a life! By that time the air in the room would be stale and stuffy and the whole atmosphere almost overwhelmingly oppressive.

I was on the morning shift and we had to get up at 4:30. But I could never wash the sleep out of my eyes, for there was no water. There was water only in the afternoon for a few hours, in a small room next to the toilets. But by then almost nobody needed water, and anyway at that time there were very few men in the barracks. The room, with five washbasins and three makeshift toilets for fifty men, opened off a dark corridor between the bedrooms. Because of the water shortage the toilets were usually filthy according to the most elementary standards of hygiene. The resulting stench penetrated into the corridor. Under these circumstances many of the men neglected the minimum demands of society. Some urinated without embarrassment against the walls of their rooms. A drain in the floor accommodated the rest.

No wonder my roommates opened their eyes in the morning with a curse, sighing *"Quelle vie!"* They weren't being theatrical.

Because of the regular absence of water most of them bought themselves a daily bottle of mineral water, and if I had wanted to shave in the morning, I would have had to use that, too.

Unwashed and unshaven, filthy in our working clothes, we drank coffee downstairs in the barracks, a big cup that we had to get at the counter. We had a wine bottle filled with coffee for lunch—the *casse-croûte*—and we also had a choice of a piece of cheese or sausage—the cheese about four inches square and about a half inch thick. We had a few bites of dry bread with our coffee and put the rest with the bottle and the cheese in the lunchbox. After that we went out into the cool morning on our way to the mine.

At 4:45 the workers who had no bicycles departed, and fifteen minutes later the others followed. Most of them wore old rags. My work pants, originally blue, had soon taken on the brown tone of the ore mud that rubbed against them every day. Over my shirt I wore a dirty jacket. It would have been an impossible chore to put something clean on every morning. The daily trip to the mine was as sad a picture as life in the workers' colony generally.

Yet I don't think it can be said that the men, either consciously or unconsciously, were deeply depressed by the strain of the daily monotony. They had grown familiar with it. They felt united by a common fate. And the daily greeting, *salut, ca va?*, or *bonjour* was friendly enough.

On the day I arrived in the colony nobody had said a word to me, but from the moment I was seen in the mine I belonged to them. This seems to be the general pattern among the miners. As soon as they share the same living and working conditions, a friendship of higher quality develops among them. This friendship is spontaneous, taken for granted, and without pretensions. They can usually count on each other in difficulties, and they help each other out without considering it a good deed.

The mine complex was a colorless place. I always wonder why buildings belonging to an industry should have to be constructed without style. If the industry can't afford to spend much, there still remain two questions to be answered. First of all, doesn't the human factor count, the joy of working which depends partly on the surroundings? And secondly, do construction costs really go up when building exteriors and interiors are planned with some regard for aesthetic effects? Not only do these expenses seem warranted—if not required—by the obligations an industry has toward its workers, but the morale among them might be improved to such an extent that the industry would profit from it. Fortunately there are a lot of industries at present which do give their workers more and more—whatever their motivations. But many can't yet shake off the heritage of the last century.

On our arrival at the mine we each received a number at the window of a small building at the entrance gate. This was to check whether all who went down came back up later. We parked our bicycles in special racks. Then we could change clothes in the shower room. But since there was no prescribed working outfit, many went down in the same clothes they were wearing on arrival.

We had to be present fifteen minutes before the descent into the mine. There was no waiting room, however. The shower room was too small for this purpose, and anyway it had to be available for workers returning from the mine. So all we could do was to wait outside, crouching on the ground or on a pile of stones until it was time to go down—regardless of weather. Meanwhile returning mine workers would give instructions to those about to go down.

A siren gave the signal to get into a train which would take us a distance of about six miles underground and to a depth of about seven hundred yards. The cars were low—we couldn't stand up in them—without windows and made entirely of iron. On the wooden benches across the cars three men could sit with an effort, squeezed like sardines in a tin; every inch of space had to be used. There was no light except from someone's mine lamp.

The mood in a car depended on little things. Sometimes hardly anybody would speak a word until the end, although it was a trip of about a half hour through the dark. It would have been hard to make oneself heard in any case because of the deafening noise of the train. Sometimes a few words were shouted back and forth or the men amused themselves by tipping off each other's helmets and throwing them in the air. But on the whole, little was said. It usually took a few hours each morning for the men to come to life. At the end of the trip we split up into groups and got further instructions from the foremen. Then we had to walk quite a distance through unlighted corridors before arriving at the place of work. Only here and there along the main tracks was there a light; on the side routes the only illumination was from our own carbide lamps.

In the iron mines, unlike the coal mines, it is quite chilly, so chilly that we got cold after a while if we didn't keep moving. The pleasant thing was that we could smoke there, for there was no gas.

Taking as a whole the circumstances in which the workers lived and the way they had to go to work, it was impossible to avoid the conclusion that they were hardly respected as human individuals by the industry that employed them. The friendship among themselves was about the only valid human element. Those who had homes and families and didn't have to live in the barracks were slightly better off. Their day started a little more humanly because the wife or the family looked after them. But in the mine and in the official work schedule they were treated as indifferently as the workers living in the barracks. Yet I never

noticed a strong revolt anywhere. They went their way, resigned
to their workers' lot.

There was, however, a latent discontent. Most of the men were
indifferent when it came to revolution, but they were open to
Communist influences because Communists made them aware of
their situation. They had long been disillusioned, however, by
Communist activity. They were men imprisoned by their fate and
all they had was an inner resistance. "This is how it is, and this
is the way it will always be." It was like a continuous experience
of inferiority.

Perhaps this is society's greatest crime against the workers, and
at the same time it makes the soil most fertile for Communism,
in which repressed human values can find a means of expression.
This is how faith in a myth starts, and this is why Communism
will find these people—even after periods of disillusion and indifference—again and again susceptible to its ideals, unless non-
Communist Europe can find effective ways to help emancipate
the workers. Social legislation is a step in the right direction—as
long as it is not so superficial as to leave the core of the problem
untouched.

4

THE chief engineer saw to it that on the first morning I went with
one of the foremen to the most modern part of the mine, the area
called Joy, after the American machines used there.

The mine was divided into three layers according to the color
of the ore and rocks: the red, the yellow and the wild yellow

(la couche rouge, la couche jaune, la couche jaune sauvage). Not
every layer lent itself readily to modern mechanization. But in
the red layer one could work with a firm ceiling and high, wide
corridors. I soon saw that there was little for me, with no technical qualifications of any kind, to do.

Everywhere it was pitch-dark. The electric lamp on my helmet
threw only a ray of light which gave the corridors with their eerie
walls a brownish hue.

At first I followed the foreman who explained things, but after
a while I stood watching a big American scraper, and he went
his own way. The scraper was a monster on wheels, like an
enormous lobster with mechanical arms that picked up the pieces
of ore loosened by explosives. Right behind the scraper stood an
American loading cart to which the ore was transferred from the
conveyor-belt of the scraper. Only two men were needed to work
the two machines. Loading was a noisy, dusty operation. It was a
strange sight—the two men silhouetted against the glow of the
lamps on their helmets. A small lighthouse beam paralleled every
movement of head or body, each time lighting up something new
in the surrounding darkness. The men were completely absorbed
in their work with a kind of conscious superiority over matter.

Like a prehistoric animal with two shining eyes, the loading
cart zoomed through the dark corridors to a kind of reservoir;
from there the ore was thrown into dump-carts passing through a
corridor on a slightly deeper level. A row of empty carts stood
ready. One man could pull the lever to load the carts and put
them into motion. This mechanization meant an enormous saving
of labor. The men who managed the machines were proud of
their work and conscious that their position in the industry was
more important than that of the other workers. It was no slave's
job. The worker derives a sense of power by suggestion from his
environment, just as the lord of a castle forms an idea of what he
"is" from the panorama of the land he owns. The rich get this
idea from their sumptuous homes and the big cars they casually
park in front of their offices or hotels.

In the Joy there was a suggestion of pride, a consciousness of being somebody in the industry and in the society that uses ore by the thousands of tons. And this suggestion took on its own aura in the spectacle of moving silhouettes, in the interplay of light and dark. For the outsider it was a spectacle, but for the participants it meant the playing of a part, unconscious but clearly seen in its effects. These workers had something indefinable about them that distinguished them from the other miners. Not that they formed a separate group or class, but they were more conscious of their individuality, prouder, more interested, more contented and happier. Yet they kept on a friendly footing with the others, who were not aware of any essential difference between these workers and themselves. They were most evidently pleased that I was fascinated by their work. Their greetings on the street became friendlier and they liked to stop and talk. I had seen them at their work and knew what they were worth. From then on I could visit them in their homes.

To what could this favorable effect of modern technology be ascribed? Not to the technology itself, for I know other mines where workers are embittered by it. I believe it depends on the way it is utilized in the industry. One can make it serve production and man, but one can also make the mistake of sacrificing man to technique.

There was a lot of water in the corridors, which didn't hinder the machines, but which forced me to neckbreaking feats just to keep moving. I had to take the lamp off my helmet to find dry spots. Once two headlights appeared in the dark and a loading cart came zooming straight at me, splashing water all over. There was a cry of "Look out, look out!" The monster carefully veered by me, and a smiling brown face winked at me in passing. I passed a side corridor where something was going on. Miners' lamps were moving like searchlights around a defective machine. A mechanic was lying on his back, repairing something. I stood still, but on the wrong side of the machine, which could have smashed me with one blow of its big steel claws.

"If you want to stay alive, come and stand over here!"

I obeyed. I jumped aside and stood watching the mechanic work.

When he had finished he looked at me with satisfaction, but at the same moment the alarm sounded. An explosive was about to be detonated, and everyone had to find a safe place. The mechanic shouted at me to follow him, and a few moments later I was with him in his work shed. The deafening explosions came. Five of them. Everything roared and rumbled. In the shed he pulled me to a place where no rocks could be loosened. He held his hands over his ears, and I followed his example. *Un, deux, trois* . . . finished? . . . *non* . . . *quatre* . . .? . . . *encore* . . . *cinq.* "Terrible," he mumbled when it was all over. Through the door of his shed I saw that the air was filled with dust and smoke. "Come here, close the door, it's no good going out there for a while." He pulled out some big diagrams and went over them with his finger. I didn't understand much of it. He was a friendly, serious man of about forty.

"You'll have to excuse me," I said, "I can only follow the main lines of what you're telling me. I'm not a technical man!"

"Is this your first day in the mine?"

"Yes."

"Apprentice?"

"Yes and no. Depends on what you want to call it. I work here because I want to know what it's like in the iron mines."

He looked at me with pity and sat down on the table, while I stood leaning against the wall.

"You don't know what you're getting into. That's nothing for you . . . are you an unskilled laborer?"

"Yes."

"Are you going to do loading?"

"Yes, why not?"

"No . . . ." He made a gesture of revulsion. "*Pauvre garçon.* Who sent you here?"

"Nobody. It was my own idea."

"No, no!" (It was as if he were trying to restrain someone from

suicide.) "I've had to do it too, but I found I couldn't. The first
weeks I was simply dead. I couldn't eat or sleep—only drink.
Fortunately I was soon put with the technical department."

"Were you able to do this kind of work straight off?"

"I was already a technician when I came to the mine."

"You like it better here?"

"At least you earn more here. But the work is dangerous and
unhealthy."

I offered him a cigarette and said: "Not a bad room you have
here."

Usually the workers and even the foremen have to find safe
places in the corridors. He made a mocking grimace.

"Nothing but a hole. They could have made it a lot cozier. Why
didn't they brighten it up a little?"

He got up to go back to work.

"Anyway, you know where I am. Come back tomorrow; I'll
show you some new types of machines."

"I don't know whether I can come back tomorrow."

"Where do you live?"

"In the barracks."

"In the barracks? You shouldn't live there." He shook his head.
"Why don't they let you live in the other building, the casino?"

I thought to myself: if everyone knows what the barracks is
like, why don't they do something about it?

"It's all right so far!" I said.

"Drop by some evening!"

"I'd like to, but what is your name?"

"Marcel. I live right near the mine. Everybody knows me.
They'll tell you where it is."

"O.K."

I continued my trip and saw men working among big tanks.
A bluish vapor hung over the earth. Liquid oxygen was being
transferred to round cylinders. The temperature of this liquid is
so low that touching it causes serious burns. A young man walked
away with one of the cylinders, and I went with him. We came

to a spot where a pneumatic drill had made holes in the rock about ten feet deep and an inch in diameter. Two men were busy filling long thin bags with sand. My friend put down the cylinder and hastily dropped cartridges filled with a kind of sawdust into the oxygen. The others started loading the holes. Quickly they pulled a cartridge out of the smoking cylinder, attached a fuse and placed the whole thing in a hole. Then followed several small bags of sand, tamped tight with a long stick. Then again a container of oxygen and again sand, and in a short time all the holes were filled. The alarm was sounded by striking an iron bar, the fuses were lit, and everyone ran.

Crouched against the wall of another corridor we waited for the explosion. It came after a few moments with a frightening thunder. We stayed in the same position for another five minutes till the effect had worn off. There was so much dust and smoke that I couldn't make anything out. Nobody had any protection. No wonder many of the boys are worried about getting silicosis. Working in dust and smoke irritates them to the point of bitterness—the same men who are so proud and friendly before such a nightmarish explosion. Soon afterward an American scraper and a loading cart appeared and began their work. Only gradually was the air purified by ventilation.

The workers started to drill another piece of rock. I kept watching.

"Want to try?" one of them asked.

It seemed rather simple. I took over the pneumatic drill. You start with a three-foot drill. After a while you pull it out and replace it with a six-foot one and finally with a ten-foot. I started with the short drill. The man pointed to the place where a hole was to be made. I put the drill at that spot and switched on the compressed air. Immediately the tool in my hands began to dance and jump away. The man who had given me the drill was amused.

"The beginning is always difficult. Here, give it back to me."

In no time at all he drilled a four-inch hole and handed me the drill again. I had to press with my thigh and the whole weight of my body. The drill shook in my hands, my thigh trembled, everything throbbed painfully. After a few minutes the pain became too much. It was unbearable. I gave back the drill.

"Pretty hard work!" I remarked.

At first the drill tears the skin of the upper leg that is pressing against it. But these men seemed to have become hardened to it, for a skilled worker drills a ten-foot hole in less than ten minutes. It is "easier" if you can drill at the level of your upper leg or your chest. The situation becomes much more critical when you have to hold the drill over your head and push it into the rock with all the strength of your muscles. No wonder that in spite of the low temperature in the mine, these men sweat like driven slaves.

About one o'clock it was time to go back. Mysteriously the little miners' lamps moved through the dark corridors. Seated on timbers, we waited for the arrival of the train. Not much was said. At about a quarter of two we were back in the daylight.

You could take a shower if you wanted to, but most of the men just washed the upper part of their bodies at the little faucets fixed in a row over a trough. They wanted to get away as soon as possible. Where to? To a colony that was so monotonous that all it could offer was boredom.

Back in the barracks we could line up and get a plateful of salad, potatoes and some meat. After that we threw ourselves on our beds. And after the worst of the fatigue had worn off there was nothing to do but to hang around or walk about a little. The men sat on the steps daydreaming—for hours. Many drank away their boredom in a bar. But the men with families couldn't afford that, and most of the bachelors were foreigners who saved their money to send home.

5

THE chief engineer of the mine was a strange individual. He was a war invalid, half paralyzed, and he walked with a cane; a young man still, with tight, grim features. Even his smile was cramped, and often it was hard to tell whether he was taking me seriously or not. His word was law, however, and whatever he said was done as a matter of course. He had heard that I was sleeping in the barracks. That seemed to create quite a stir! When I appeared at the mine the second day, he beckoned to me.

"Where do you sleep?"

"In the barracks."

"Who arranged that? They're crazy." And with a friendly look of understanding: "I'll see to it that they put you somewhere else. This will be your last day there!"

"Don't worry about me. I wanted it myself."

"Why?"

"I prefer to live with the workers."

He gave me an inscrutable look.

"Well, it's your own business. Yesterday you were in the *couche rouge*. You want to go there again or to another part?"

"It was very interesting, but I don't think I could work there."

"Why not?"

"It's all mechanized and I'm not a technician."

"You mean you want to work yourself?"

"As much as possible, yes."

"You're out of your mind! You may want to know the problems of the mine and of the miners, but that's no reason to go and work yourself. Besides, the miners have only one problem . . . ."

"Really?"

"Of course, you can take my word for it, it's only wages they're interested in, only wages. That's all that counts. And if they're not satisfied, well . . . ." He made a movement as if to kick someone out the door. "But you have a blank check, you can do as you like."

I wanted to go, but he held me back.

"Come and have dinner with me sometime!"

I didn't quite know what to say.

"Fine. We'll be seeing one another," he replied to my silence.

How could I ignore this invitation? Could I tell him why I would rather not accept?

He signaled to a foreman to go along with me. I couldn't understand what they said.

The foreman's name was Vladimir; he was a Pole. He had come to France with his parents as a very small child, but he had never wished to become naturalized. He was a cheerful, amiable man of about forty. That morning he would first show me the section he supervised—he had fifty or sixty men under him—and afterward we would talk. On our way to the mine Vladimir grumbled about the electric lamp on his helmet.

"Worthless, the damn thing."

"Why?"

"Because you get a ray only in one direction. You can't see anything around you. The carbide lamps were better for that."

The miners had started to buttress a corridor. It was a difficult spot and they didn't know how to go about it. But Vladimir did. He took the drill himself, made a few holes in no time, and placed the beams correctly. He was a sympathetic fellow who didn't give orders without lending a hand when there was a difficult job to do. He had a lot of experience, for he had worked in the mine since he was quite young. His section was not mechanized. The ore layer was too dangerous for high, wide corridors to be constructed. The work in this part was much heavier than in the mechanized section I had seen the previous day. But I could sense that the men liked Vladimir.

The workers were divided into groups of three. The most skilled worker handled the pneumatic drill, the other two had to load the chunks of ore into the dump-carts by hand. The place where the three men worked was called a *chantier*.

When we had gone through Vladimir's section in all directions and the men had been checked at their posts, we came to a *chantier* full of ore waiting to be loaded. The previous shift had left it behind. That was all right, for in this way the new shift could make its quota more easily. Apparently that's what the loaders had in mind, for they worked furiously, sweating like horses. On top of the ore pile the driller was busy making new holes. There was enough work for a helper to be useful, and I stayed. The introductions were short, businesslike and friendly.

"Hans."

"Erich."

"Frans," I said.

They were two young fellows of about twenty-five, the first a German, the second a Pole. The driller would not be distracted, but kept on working. They took big blocks in their muscular arms and threw them in the dump-carts. I followed their example. It was bending and lifting without let-up, and soon my whole body was perspiring. Chunks that were too big to be lifted were first split with the pneumatic drill. Waste was taken care of with a shovel. Erich patted me on the back with sympathy and said smiling: "Frans!" All three of us were in good spirits. Little was said. We would have had to shout, anyway.

As soon as the cart was filled, lamps were hooked around its edges. We chose our spots and began to push—first with our arms, for the corridor was smooth for a while, then with our heads and sometimes our chests too, or with our backs when the path went upward. The cart held two and a half tons. Sometimes we had to pull it back and put a piece of wood against the wheels, and then push again till we came to the main corridor, where the train was waiting for the full carts. Halfway back, Hans was already getting an empty cart from a side corridor. At the end of the line we paused to catch our breath for a moment, leaning against the wall, unable to utter a word. We wiped our wet faces till they were a streaky brown, and then started the run back. Hans was the first to begin loading again. The object was to fill as many dump-carts as possible, for the tonnage determined the wages, which were based on achievement, above a minimum wage. The carts were numbered with chalk and weighed and recorded above ground.

It was a pace and a routine that could hardly be called human, and when after a few hours I was completely exhausted, I wondered if they were mad. But they weren't. Everywhere in the non-mechanized part of the mine people worked like that—with wages as the stimulus. Was the engineer really right when he said that nothing else mattered to them?

The boys saw that I was worn out.

"It's always like that in the beginning," they said. "You'll get used to it. Take it easy."

Marcel had predicted it. I had thought he exaggerated. But I couldn't hold a drill for five minutes or load for an hour without being exhausted.

The driller had finished with the holes. Together we filled cartridges with sand. The container of liquid oxygen was pulled out, the holes filled, the fuses prepared and lit . . . and we ran for safety. We took a breather. But after only five minutes we had to get back again.

It was stifling hot in the *chantier,* and we could hardly see each other. But there was no mercy. The work went on at the same tempo. After four hours there was a fifteen-minute break for lunch.

We sat together on some cases along the tracks leading to corridors further on, where we had hung our things on a nail. We laughed at meaningless jokes and drank cold black coffee with a

hunk of butterless bread and a piece of cheese, given us that
morning at the barracks. Hans was a witty fellow, who made fun
of everything.

Vladimir was sitting with us. He looked at what we were
eating.

"Damn it, you always get the same old thing. A little cube of
cheese with some dry bread. It's a shame. That boss of yours is
doing fine by you. No need to ask where he gets the money to
have two houses built and to keep a motorcycle. He knows how
to feather his nest. I knew him when he was just an ordinary
worker here. He worked hard, but that barracks has turned into
an unexpected gold mine for him. It may belong to the company,
but he is making plenty buying the stuff and making smart deals
with the suppliers!"

Erich only listened. He didn't live in the barracks. Hans
laughed and added to Vladimir's comment: "Salad—potatoes—
macaroni—and a little meat, today, tomorrow, the day after
tomorrow, and so on."

We were sitting in a dangerous spot. The corridor went downward about seventy-five feet in a steep curve. When the dump-
carts arrived at the beginning of the slope, they were tied to a
metal cable and let down slowly. But sometimes the cable broke
or, because of some oversight, the carts started their descent
before they were tied to the cable. With tremendous speed they
would plunge down into the rocks of the corridor below, where
the train was supposed to meet them. Unlucky the man who just
happened to pass at that moment. That's what we talked about
during our meal. A few days later I witnessed just such an event,
fortunately one without injury to anyone.

We went back to work. A chunk of ore broke in two when I
picked it up. It had a crack that I hadn't noticed. My finger
slipped between the halves and my hand turned into a dirty
mess of blood and mud. But I didn't feel any pain. A first-aid kit
took care of it right away.

Watching my friends, I could see that the pace of the work

was gradually slackening. They were exhausted—knocked out. We had loaded fifteen dump-carts, or about thirty-five tons, and had blasted three times.

In the train we sat shoulder to shoulder, squeezed together. "I hope there's a little more room for us in heaven," someone remarked. What a day! And to know that for those people every day is like that. For ten, twenty years. Then they are used up. Miners generally don't get old; quite a few die prematurely of silicosis.

Going back to the barracks Erich caught up with me. We cycled on together.

"Tired?" I asked.

"*Oh oui!*" he sighed. He didn't seem as cheerful as during work.

"I guess you sleep half the afternoon!"

"*Oh oui, c'est la vie!* That's life!"

I had to laugh. "What is life? To sleep?"

"Yes, wear yourself out, eat and sleep!"

"Is there nothing going on in the village?"

"There are two movie houses, so you can go twice a week, there are cafés, there are girls. And you can go into town. There's a little more there, but not too much. Pretty dead on the whole."

"Have you been working long in the mine?"

"Five years."

"You like it?"

"Well, what else can you do? That's life!"

"How do you mean?"

"Well, what else can you do as a worker? You've got to take the work you can get. It's the same thing everywhere. It's a question of earning money, here or somewhere else."

"Don't you have a chance for promotion?"

He replied, discouraged: "I am a Pole. The better jobs are for the French. You always remain a foreigner. That's why I couldn't get into the mining school."

"But there are Poles and other foreigners who do have good jobs in the mine, aren't there?"

"Yes, but those are special cases. No . . . ." He made a gesture of you-don't-have-to-tell-me-anything.

Erich lived close by the barracks.

"What are you doing this afternoon?" he asked me when we arrived.

"I don't know yet."

"If you like, we can go cycling or swimming."

"All right."

"I'll come by to see if you're in. Otherwise, see you tomorrow."

6

I WENT into the dining room, took off my knapsack and got a plate for some macaroni soup. Macaroni soup every day because of the many Italians! I looked for an empty seat. Halfway into the room I saw Hans. He signaled and shouted: "Frans!" I signaled back and maneuvered my plate through the crowd to where he was sitting. I sat down beside him. "Hya, Frans." He gave me a slap on the shoulder. Four of us sat together: Hans, who was from Munich; Klaus, a slender, well-brought-up boy from Berlin; and Max, a friend from Breslau. Three blond Germanic types. They lived together in one room in one of the houses belonging to the barracks.

"Are you coming back tomorrow, Frans?" asked Hans.

"That depends on the boss."

He told his buddies how I had worked that morning. It was

funny. I doubted whether he could have two serious thoughts in a row.

Klaus was much more serious. He looked as if he came from a better class. He sighed.

"You can't call that work any more. It just kills you. When I first came here . . . ." He made a gesture describing exhaustion. "I can't take it. I'll get out as soon as I can."

"When will that be?"

"At Christmas. Then I'll go to Berlin on leave, and they'll never see me back!"

"We made about forty tons this morning," Hans exaggerated.

"Yes, you can do that where you are. You should be with us. Water and no air! Try to make forty tons there!" Klaus said bitterly.

We went to get our potatoes. Hans ordered and paid for a glass of wine for me. He put it down in front of me.

"You're coming again tomorrow!"

"I don't know!"

"Yes, you are. It'll be okay with Vladi."

At the end of the meal we were joined by Polski, from Lorraine, who also spoke German.

"Hiya, Polski!"

"Have you met?" Hans asked me.

"No, not yet."

"Well, better look out for him. He's a terror around here."

I was indeed to find out soon that Polski commanded much respect among his co-workers. They called him *le bombardier,* the bomber. He was the train driver and could thunder through the mine corridors with ominous speed. Yet he was no boaster, but rather a sensitive man, and usually drunk. But when he wanted to bawl someone out he called a spade a spade.

Hans ordered another round of wine for everyone. Polski offered cigarettes and only then answered Hans' remark in a very serious tone. "They are afraid of me . . . but they can't say I'm not a good buddy to everyone."

He, too, ordered another round. I declined, but he made it clear that I was not to be silly, that I had to drink. Polski was not married, earned good money, and could be relied upon for help when someone was in need. Hans again told how I had worked in the mine for the first time that morning, and in his *chantier*.

"If you want to see how the transportation works, you can go with me one morning," Polski said.

"Oh," Hans exclaimed. "Then you'll thank your lucky stars if you come back alive in the afternoon!"

"It's all very well, but how can I manage it?"

Polski made a sign of "Just leave it to me."

We got up. Hans signaled me to come with him. We crossed the street to where he and the others lived. A step was missing from the stairs; if one were not careful, he would fall into the cellar.

Hans turned on his radio and Max his, both to the same station. They didn't have to support anyone and could afford the luxury. Soon all three were lying stretched out on their beds, and I was sitting on the edge of Klaus' bed. The conversation was about many things—about the war, about the dirty mess in the barracks and in the shower room at the mine, about the new barracks they had known before they came here. Modern installations were something quite different! The work in the iron mines was heavy, much harder than in the coal mines. Coal miners usually couldn't stand the work in the iron pits very long.

Hans was a miner by profession, the others out of necessity. Hans liked the work. He told how he had also helped drill tunnels through mountains. But most of all he'd like to get back to the coal mines, where he had become a skilled worker.

What in heaven's name had possessed me to come and work here? they wanted to know.

"To get to know the iron mines."

"Aren't there any iron mines in Holland?"

"No, only coal mines."

"Wouldn't there be work for me in the Dutch mines?" Hans inquired.

"Perhaps, if you weren't too friendly with the Party under Hitler."

"I was only in the ordinary Wehrmacht."

"You could try."

"Are there pretty girls in Holland?"

"Same as everywhere!"

"In two weeks there's going to be a fair here. Man . . . ." He slapped me on the shoulder—he was sitting opposite from me by this time—"The four of us will go there. At night there's dancing. The mine gives us two days off!"

The others didn't react at all. They were just lying there, listening lazily.

"That's all very well for you, you're making good money. But I have hardly a penny," I said.

He replied with a grand gesture: "Don't worry about money. I've got plenty. We're going together. Last year at the fair I went through forty thousand francs in two days."

"Not bad. What did you do to manage that?"

Cheerfully he told us: "Oh Frans, I'm a pig, you know."

"You are?"

"When I was a little boy I was already looking under girls' skirts. My mother always told me I would come to no good. If you ever need a dog . . . If you ever need a dog . . . ."

"Then what?"

"Think of me!"

"Okay."

Everybody laughed.

"My God, that was something last year. I was all by myself . . . and I was drinking away all my money in a beauty of a bar. I was alone at first—but soon I picked up a damn beautiful girl, a blonde. And did we dance together!"

He got up and danced in perfect pantomime.

"'And now we're going to bed,' she said. My God, I've never slept in such a classy room. I was crazy about it. I was crazy about everything—about the food, the drink, about her . . . . She had beautiful eyes and beautiful hair. We kept up the party in

our room for a while . . . we kissed . . . ." He was completely
engrossed in his story and played it out for us like a first-rate
actor.

"Then I said: 'Let's get undressed . . . .' We undressed completely . . . I took her in my arms . . . oh, wonderful . . . I carried
her through the room . . . and we slept together like in paradise.
In bed I had to promise her to do it again the next day. But the
next day I disappeared. Yes, Frans, we're going to do the same
thing this year, together. Don't worry about money. We're really
going to celebrate!"

His story was finished. I got up slowly and said: "I'm going."

"Why?"

"Erich is supposed to come and get me. We're going swimming
or cycling."

"Oh, he'll come here."

"At any rate I have to go and shave."

"If Erich doesn't turn up, come back here!"

I went by Erich's house to find out what was going on. He had
gone, nobody knew where. Now it was my turn to stretch out on
my bed.

Strange feelings assailed me about Hans. A libertine and yet a
decent fellow. How many were there like him? These things
weren't talked about openly except among friends. Now I belonged in that category. How could I maintain my status if I
could never join the conversation on that topic? Not that I didn't
have anything to say on the subject. I knew enough about what
is going on in the world. But that wasn't the question. You had to
speak from experience, and either not care about morals or simply
have no morals at all. Was Hans so much worse than others only
because no God or commandment existed for him? Why did I
feel so ill at ease, when the same things did not upset me in the
confessional or when they were treated academically? Perhaps
there is the same difference between the abstract knowledge of
sin and the committing of sin as between knowledge of the
workers' world and the actual living in it. It's the same and yet
different. The latter is alive, the former a skeleton.

Why be surprised about the living thing when I knew from the skeleton what it must be? Yet the living thing is richer. It is knowledge plus experience. They may correspond, but they are different. I felt strange and yet I knew I was where I wanted to be.

I went to shave, for there was water. The boredom in the barracks was palpable. A few boys sat dreaming on the steps in front of the house. Others were asleep. The rest were in the mine or elsewhere.

When I went out a few hours later, my friends from across the street emerged at the same moment.

"Hi, Frans!"

"Where are you going?"

"Just to the village, to have a drink somewhere. Come along!"

I joined them, walking the way they did, with my hands in my pockets. But Hans couldn't pass a girl at a window without joking with her. It appeared that he was quite well known everywhere. He lagged behind. We waited a few times, but finally his friends had had enough. "Let's not wait for him. He'll enjoy himself."

We drank a glass of beer somewhere, after that a vermouth, and finally a Pernod. It's the custom among workers that each stands a round.

"Watch out for the Pernod," they warned me. "It's so strong that it makes you wild, even at night in your sleep."

At dinner Hans was back. The meal was chaotic and noisy as always. Hans treated us to wine again. If I were to eat often with him, I would never be able to escape that.

I told about the dog that had torn my trouser leg.

"Give the damn animal such a kick that he won't do it again!"

"But maybe he wouldn't let me pass alive!"

"Come and sleep with us. We'll get another bed and everything will be fine."

With some effort a fourth bed could indeed have been fitted in their room. All other rooms accommodated four men. But the boss had decided otherwise. A bed had become free in the barracks, and it was designated for me.

After dinner Hans took us to a bar in the neighborhood. We found Polski there, already slightly high. He was sitting with some other men. He signaled without saying anything and pointed to some chairs nearby.

"Nothing for me, I had a lot to drink today," I said.

"What are you drinking?" he asked, ignoring my remark. I was sitting next to him, and with the exaggerated emotions of someone not quite sober he grabbed my arm and shook his head as if to underline what he was going to say.

"Pal . . . ."

I waited.

"Pal . . . if you want to be a good pal, you have to drink."

The necessary rounds of beer, Triple Sec, Cointreau and other stuff were put in front of me in succession. If I declined, I just got the same as the others were drinking. And then I had to stand my own round! Polski began to relate his heroic feats.

"Yes, my friend . . . be a good friend to everyone! Then they respect you . . . !"

He became impressed with himself.

"I'm a good friend . . . even though they're afraid of me . . . If you need anything, just come to Polski . . . . They respect me . . . ." (with a broad gesture) "all of 'em . . . and I want to be respected."

He was almost crying.

"The other day all of us were almost killed by the train he was driving," Hans joked.

Now Polski was really crying. But after a moment he began to talk again, full of emotion.

"Come on and tell the story, Polski!"

"We were driving at full speed . . . yes, full speed . . . and . . . then I noticed that the brakes weren't working. God almighty." He hid his head in his arms on the table. "We were going to be smashed to pieces. I couldn't warn a soul, not even my pals in the little cars. The foreman was sitting next to me. 'What are we going to do?' he asks. 'Jump off the locomotive?' And I says to

him, 'If the men are going to die, Polski is going with 'em.' He
began to cry again. 'Then we'll go together, pal.' Yes, that's what
he said. It's the worst thing that ever happened to me. There were
a few hundred men in the train. I turned off the power. Would
the last slope slow us down enough . . .? Thank God, yes . . . ."

Polski was utterly shaken by this story; he ordered another
round for all of us, and then, once more overwhelmed by his
feelings, he buried his head in his arms. The others were impressed, too.

"In the mine you're never sure of your life," someone remarked.

"Well, that's the risk we take," Hans said simply. "Do you
know that poem about the mine?"

"What poem?"

"By that miner from Cologne. Beautiful! Death in the mine!
Just an ordinary miner, you know, but a masterpiece. With music,
too."

"Sing it, Hans!"

And Hans began to sing, with a voice loud enough to be heard
in town. Sentimental, and with effects. There was a dead silence.

"I've known quite a few pals who are dead and buried now,"
said Polski. "That's life!"

Jumping from one subject to another, he took my arm and said
again emphatically: "If you need anything, come to Polski. Since
my mother died, I've got nobody to care for. Money has no value,
only friendship."

"When did your mother die?"

"It'll be a year next Monday."

"Monday," Hans said, "we'll all go to church with you!"

Two women, not exactly beauties, came and sat with us. Beer
was ordered for them. They asked for a cigarette. When one of
them got up and bent over the table to get a light, Hans boldly
put his arm between her legs as if to lift her. "Frans, do you want
her?" he asked. She laughed. I said nothing. They talked some
more about things that didn't matter. Then we left.

"Can you understand," Klaus asked me, "how the men almost
murder each other here for a woman like that?"

I shrugged my shoulders.

"Good night."

"Good night."

The street was blue-black in the night. Deserted like a village on the moon.

It was almost eleven o'clock. A few Italians were still sitting in the barracks dining room. They were from the afternoon shift and had just returned. One of them sang parts from the litany of Our Lady in Latin. Perhaps not so much from devotion as because of the melody—at any rate as if it were the most ordinary thing in the world. In another part of the room others answered with *Ora pro nobis*. Perhaps, in spite of the odd surroundings, the place wasn't entirely devoid of devotion. For the most part, the Italians wore crosses or medals openly. Often a picture of the Virgin Mary or of a saint would hang over their beds. Nobody objected to that, not even the most fanatic Communists.

I went up the creaking stairs to my new room and my new roommates. Two of them were already lying on their beds. They smiled when I came in. "Good evening." The room smelled of wet earth and dried sweat. It looked grimy. Working clothes were hanging from a shelf.

"Are you on the morning shift too?" I asked.

"No."

I undressed and put the alarm clock on the floor beside my bed.

"Don't hit me when it goes off tomorrow morning at four-thirty, will you?"

"Oh, no!"

I turned off the light—"Good night"—crawled under the blankets and said my evening prayer.

The next morning Vladimir put me with the workers who take care of the maintenance of the corridors, and who do not work in the *chantier*. It's a mixture of light and heavy work. These people don't get the chance to earn as much as the drillers and loaders. They have to be satisfied with a fixed wage and from time to time

a bonus, when they have to work under particularly difficult
conditions. They have a hard time making ends meet.

I had to carry rails. There were two of us. It was not an easy
job! My partner didn't seem to feel anything, and I didn't let
him know that sometimes I could hardly bear it because of the
pain in my shoulder. The pace was inexorable. I would have
liked to say that it was too much for me, but the thought came
to me that others had had to start like that, too, and that they
couldn't complain, either, if they ever wanted to get anywhere.
What's so bad about carrying rails? Don't let on . . . just go on
carrying them . . . walk in a steady rhythm, as if nothing were
the matter. And then go back again immediately to get more.

Among us there was an old worker who didn't really do anything—and I didn't begrudge him the fact that he took it easy,
for he was much too old. But as soon as the foreman approached
he became suddenly very active. A worker doesn't like to be considered inferior or only at half-strength. Once, when I was sent
to help a worker who was used to working alone, he accepted
only under protest, for he regarded the help as an insult to his
own capacity. The workers are proud of what they do. Sometimes
I would see the disappointment in the face of a certain worker
if I assured him that I was meeting him for the first time, while
he informed me that I had already seen him doing such-and-such
work. So it had made no impression on me! Their achievements
meant so much to them that it hurt when I didn't seem to
recognize them.

Once my bicycle had a flat and I had to walk to the barracks.
Polski caught up with me, got off his bike and walked the rest of
the way with me. He talked again about friendship and about
being alone in the world. Within a year he had lost his mother
and his sister. His sister had died quite suddenly in a hospital
outside Filondange. But he had seen to it that she was buried
here.

"That was a to-do! The priest wouldn't bury her because she

hadn't received the last rites! Fancy refusing to bury a Christian!
She never went to church. According to the priest, we could
bury her where we pleased as long as the Church had nothing to
do with it. Then I let him know he was dealing with Polski. I
said to him: 'If you refuse to bury a Christian at the Catholic
cemetery, we'll do it ourselves. By force, if necessary.' Then he
got frightened, for he knew I would do it. 'Polski,' he said, 'you're
not a bad guy,' and so she was buried here. And decently, too,
for I insisted on that.

"I'm not a bad guy . . . ! I'll tell you that I don't go to church
often, but when I do, Polski can pray like the best of 'em. We're
all human beings, the priest too, and I don't condemn anybody.
But if they want to treat a Christian like a dog—and after his
death at that—they'll know that they're dealing with Polski!"

7

I HAD been told that France differs from region to region in matters of religion, and that therefore the workers' communities
differ, too. Gradually I began to doubt it, for the workers' community in Filondange had little to do with the surrounding area.
It was centered almost entirely on the mine.

Of the 822 workers in that mine in June 1951, only 376 were
French as against 446 foreigners. Among the foreigners were 12
North Africans, 17 Luxembourgers, 10 Germans, 213 Italians,
159 Poles, 17 Yugoslavs and 18 from other countries.

In reality there was little contact with the village of Filondange.
The workers were a community in themselves. A strange, artificial community at that, for they had little feeling of solidarity

outside their work. The only ties which kept them together were those of work and of "class." Only these gave the workers a feeling of belonging. There was no unity of thought or of custom. There was no local tradition such as is still found in the naturally formed villages of France. Therefore one cannot expect the same religious feeling in a workers' colony as in the region around it. The proportion of practising Catholics in the village is different from that of the colony. I have found this to be true wherever the workers form a separate colony, and there is little reason to suppose that colonies in non-religious regions differ from those in devout areas.

The workers live a very isolated existence within their work- and class-community. Their friendship usually boils down to doing or not doing something together. It's no more than a bond originating in their work and extended through the fact that they stand up for each other. But it seldom develops into friendship in the deeper sense of the word. The solidarity of the workers is often touching, and at the same time one senses within it the desolation of the lonely individual. The hunger for appreciation, sympathy and love is great, and has its effect on the other classes. But on the other hand it does not have the effect of producing the society of brotherhood that would be ideal. The worker is not really involved as a person in his own community. Is it perhaps because love is essentially an individual thing? I don't think so. It would appear so, even outside the workers' class. But that is not the essence of love, certainly not of Christian love. The population of an industrial community is held together by work and by class feeling, but this population is more impermanent than the population of any other village. For workers come and go. Among workers of the same nationality there is indeed a greater sense of solidarity—sometimes they even organize their own social circle—but this, too, is modified by constant changes and by the fact that even people of the same nationality meet only by the accident of working in a certain industry and remain essentially strangers to each other.

The elements of hopelessness in the worker's life in the big industries are manifold. But the lack of national unity is certainly one of them. This is all the more sad because workers are forced to get jobs abroad by sheer necessity, though they still have their own national orientation. Moreover, a foreigner does not assimilate as easily and is in constant fear of being sent back on the slightest provocation.

Marcel, the technician I had met in the modern part of the mine, lived in one of the new houses the mine had just built—beautiful, spacious homes, like those in which a worker in Holland might live. He had furnished the living room soberly but tastefully, with new furniture and a wide couch. On the dresser stood a beautiful hand-made copper sailboat. He had a good radio. In short, he had a cozy home. He loved music and played the violin.

"Hello," he called when I came in, "how's life?"

"All right . . . ."

He took me by the arm. "Sit down." I did.

"And how are you getting on in the barracks?"

"All right. . . ."

His wife poured wine for us.

"You're not short of anything?"

"Oh, no. . . ."

"If we can be of help with anything, just say so!"

He looked at me with concern, as if he didn't believe me. Strange, how irrational human sympathy is.

"Thanks, but I don't need any more than a place to eat and sleep."

He laughed. "Who's going to wash your clothes?"

"Well . . . I don't know yet."

"*Eh bien,* bring 'em here. My wife can do it."

"No . . . ."

"Yes!" said his wife, who was making coffee.

And that's what happened.

Many times we talked till late at night about the mine, about
modern technology, about music, about many other things, and
also about religion. And every time we made a date for another
evening.

"Are you a Catholic?" he asked me once.

"Yes, aren't you?"

"Baptized."

"And as for the rest?"

"For the rest, I don't believe."

"Why not?"

"I think the whole Church business is rather sickening. People
go to church to see and be seen. And the money-grabbing they
do! Saint Anthony here and another saint there. I think the
Church has very little to do with religion. Do you go to church?"

"Yes."

"I do believe that God exists. I don't know whether or not
Christ is God. I find that hard to accept. I think it's much more
probable that he was just an extraordinary human being."

"Well, I go to church because I believe in Christ, too."

"But what about that horrible business? Doesn't that disgust
you?"

"What does it matter? If the Church were nothing but that, I
wouldn't go either!"

"But that's all it is!"

"I don't believe so. It's difficult to judge whether what seems
like formalism is actually only formalism and nothing else. It's
the same with selfishness, hypocrisy and greed."

"I don't see the difference."

"Let's suppose that it's all true; even then it is only a detail
that doesn't affect the true Church."

"How do you explain that?"

"The Church is more than that!"

"More in what way?"

"I wouldn't know what the meaning of life is, if God didn't
exist. I wouldn't understand, either, why I exist. Why I was born

and why I am sitting here now. My father and mother might ask
themselves the same questions."

"But I do believe in God!"

"And I believe, moreover, that God has not left us to fate."

"Hm."

"For what purpose do you repair a machine? To get it working
again. And you're happy when you succeed. Then you can relax.
You get paid for it, too, so you can buy the things you need and
like. Your work is in the service of your happiness. But now I ask
you, when is a man happy?"

"When he has what he wants."

"When he has what he wants? Do you have everything you
want? Is there anyone in the world who has everything he
wants?"

"As long as you have enough money."

"Is that what you think? Then why do the rich always look for
something new? Why do you go to the movies? To see something
outside your daily experience. But if you have been looking at
movies for six hours straight, you are tired of them and want
something else again. I don't think there is anything in this world
that can make man perfectly happy. And yet he wants to be
perfectly happy. Isn't that strange?"

"I've never thought about that. But we were talking about the
Church."

"Have a little patience. I only wanted to tell you that I don't
go to church to get disgusted."

"Oh," he said amicably, "I never thought you would."

"I only wanted to ask what the meaning of life is if everyone
seeks happiness without ever finding it the way he wants. Now
I believe that man will never find this happiness until after this
life, with God."

"I can go along with that."

"But how exactly do you believe it?"

"I don't know."

"How can you reach God?"

"By dying."

"How do you know?"

"I just believe it."

"But why do you know it and why do you believe it? Who told you?"

He shrugged his shoulders, smiling. He had been listening with wonder.

"I know and believe the same as you, but because I think that God has not left us in the lurch."

"What do you mean by that?"

"I mean that if people try to solve the riddle of their own existence, they will get all confused. If God hadn't said anything about the origin and meaning of life, I wouldn't know how it would end except in death. So that would be the end of a life that never found what it was looking for. That would be very strange indeed. But God isn't strange at all. He has given us an answer to the riddles of our existence and revealed the meaning of our life. And because we cannot reach God by ourselves He has given us the power we need to reach Him, which is grace. He has also revealed to us how we must live to fulfill the purpose of creation. Now the Church was founded in order to give people this knowledge and tell them of this grace. And they can hang up as many offering boxes in church as they like, but that doesn't affect the real meaning of the Church, unless the money is given and spent in the true spirit of brotherly love."

"But the Church was founded by Christ, not by God!"

"Yes, but I believe that Christ *is* God! The Church is God's means of saving sinners, and a Church without sinful people in it is therefore impossible on this earth. And the Church is holy because it is Christ among us. You have to look at it realistically."

"I never looked at it that way. I was always annoyed by everything that calls itself church. The way you tell it it's a different matter, of course. But I'm surprised how much you know about those things!"

"I studied it a little. It's worthwhile, I think."

"It's impressive!"

Someone came limping in through the front door.

"Hi, Lucien!"

I was introduced to him. He was Marcel's best friend, a war veteran with a stiff leg, on which he walked painfully. He threw himself into a chair and began to talk with a beautiful French accent. A warm-hearted boy.

"What had possessed me to come and work here," he asked.

"That's what I asked him, too," said Marcel.

How did I like France?

Beautiful!

Had I been in Strasbourg?

"No, but I have to go there next week for my passport."

"Then you must visit the cathedral, something unique, with all the saints in the portico, St. Peter and whatever the others are called."

"We were just talking about the Church," said Marcel.

Lucien told a miraculous tale about a rider who had thrown himself down on the rocks, and about the devil who played a part in this. All in the neighborhood of Strasbourg. I simply must see that. The hoof-prints could still be seen in the rocks—the same rocks that were used to build the cathedral.

"Oh, come on," Marcel said, "you believe all that?"

"Have you got a better explanation?"

We laughed.

I had often seen Lucien in the lamp-storage section of the mine, but I had never met him personally. After that evening he always handed me my lamp with a smile and asked, "Everything all right?" Once in a while I would meet him in the casino, and he would always treat me to something. He never gave me the chance to pay for him. Once I visited his home with Marcel. He was married and lived in one of the drab older houses. The interior looked considerably poorer than Marcel's place. Everything was done in the kitchen. Because he worked above ground, he earned a great deal less than the underground workers. Anyway, Marcel was one of the best-paid workers in the entire mine. He was an excellent craftsman and often had to help outside his regular hours.

Vladimir lived in a block where the houses had front yards. The appearance was more cheerful, although the house itself did not differ from the others in the colony.

When I arrived on my bicycle, he was sitting on the gate talking to some men.

"Hello, Vladimir." I slowed down and waved.

"Hello," he said, coming towards me, "where are you going?"

"Nowhere, I'm just riding around."

"Come in!"

I got off the bicycle. "I really ought to make the acquaintance of the wife of my boss!"

He laughed.

"You don't think so? I think it's very important," I said.

"You should see my boys!"

"Do they speak Polish?"

"A little."

His wife was doing the dishes, and she dried her hands on her apron before greeting me. When we sat down she went back to her work.

"Just the right weather for a vacation!" I remarked.

"If you can take one!"

"Aren't you entitled to a couple of weeks a year?"

"Yes, if it's convenient to the bosses. We can't all go at the same time. It's quite possible that I won't be able to get away before the winter!"

"That would be a shame!"

"Nobody cares about that. Still, I'd like to apply for my vacation pretty soon."

"Will you go anywhere?"

"I? Where can you go if you have no money? To my family, perhaps? They live in Verdun. It's the same there as here. I'll tell

you how it is with us: you work yourself to death in the mine for
the whole year and then you are bored to death in your own
home for two weeks. You tell me what in God's name there is to
do here. Nothing. You know what we are good for? To make it
possible for others to have a good time!"

He was bitter, and talked with clenched fists. He banged his
head against the wall behind him and began to unburden his
heart.

"They all get richer from us, they all take advantage of us. And
what about us? We're nothing but suckers. The butcher, the
baker, the grocer—they're glad to serve us as long as they can
make a profit. How else can they afford cars? But when there is
a strike, when things have gone too far and we protest, and when
finally nobody has any money left, then they're not around. Ah,
yes! That's the way it is. There's nothing we can do about it.
The big shots enjoy themselves at the expense of others who are
willing to take a beating. That's life!"

"That's life!" A saying one hears again and again. A kind of
resignation to fate.

Vladimir's wife had finished her work; she poured some wine
and came and sat with us. The boys came running in, were told
to shake hands with me, and ran out again.

"Is Poland a beautiful country?" I asked.

"Poland? I should say! I've never wanted to become a naturalized Frenchman. In Poland people still know what religion is,
but here in France. . . . Over there they used to make barefoot
pilgrimages!"

Another Pole came in.

"*Bonjour.*" He sat down.

"You should see Christmas and Easter in Poland!" Vladimir
went on. "Once I was invited for Easter by some Poles here. Before dinner there was a whole ceremony of singing and praying,
and we had to kiss one another three times and say: 'May God
fulfill all your wishes'!"

"In Poland itself they probably celebrate even more."

Vladimir made a grand gesture to indicate how wonderful it was.

"You remember last Christmas?" said the other Pole. "Fantastic, how we celebrated that. I was so tipsy I couldn't even find the door of the church at night. Only when the Mass was finished I discovered that I was sitting right on the steps."

Vladimir laughed at his friend. He himself hardly drank at all.

The first Sunday in town I went to church. It was full. Alsace-Lorraine has no need of missionaries. A considerable percentage of the population is practising. A procession in full regalia paraded solemnly through the center aisle. The sermon was literally and figuratively over the heads of the people. It was pure drawing-room theology, without any contact with real life. I thought to myself: what if Marcel, Vladimir, Hans, Klaus and Polski were sitting here, and all the others who get up in the morning, sweat it out in the mine, are bored the rest of the day, and go to bed again? Would it give them one spark of happiness? Would the greatness of life with God become clear to them? I doubted it. No wonder they stayed away.

But the people listened patiently.

The following Sunday I went to another town, farther away, to be able to say Mass. The text of the Psalms, of the New Testament, and of the entire liturgy of the Mass meant more to me than usual. "*Iudica me, Deus, et discerne causam meam . . .*", I prayed in the name of my friends and of all people, *causa mea*.

I looked up Gérard Nilence's family.

"How are you, Father?"

I had to get used to "Father" again.

The kitchen door opened: "How are you, Father?"

The living-room door opened: "How are you, Father?"

Gérard, an Alsatian, was businesslike, and so was Jean. They were both concerned with the workers' world without being romantic about it, for they dealt with it every day.

"Do you get the impression," Gérard asked me during lunch,

"that boys and girls behave as freely with each other here as in Alsace?"

"How do they behave in Alsace?"

"There it's nothing unusual for boys and girls to have sexual intercourse before marriage. They don't make a secret of it. Their families know it and talk as if it's the most natural thing in the world."

"I only know that the boys do as they please and that the girls don't object. But life in the miners' colony is different from the village: everyone goes his own way. It's hard to know how many boys and girls do this kind of thing. At any rate there's no public opinion that prevents them. But that's no proof that everyone is doing it. I just don't know. At least they don't brag about it."

"And the married men?"

"I think that in general husband and wife are faithful to each other. A man doesn't often go after someone else's wife. But I wouldn't know whether they have a girl outside the colony now and then. We shouldn't dramatize what we don't know. At any rate it's not the topic of the day, and I'm not after gossip. I do know they're good people who lead difficult lives. They're people of flesh and blood, but not perverted; they're much too simple for that."

I took the bus back to the mine. To the left and right I saw nothing but industrial plants and more mines. Young men sauntered along the road or sat day-dreaming on the steps. They forgot themselves in their work, but outside of it they lived without much perspective, and on the impressions of the moment.

I saw dirty houses. Everything about workers seems stigmatized—their houses and their streets, their clothes, their hands and their faces. The whole world depends on them, yet no one would think so! In an hour I would have to stand in line for my food, plate in hand.

Yet I loved those men, hard as the rock they worked in, but like children inside; those men thrown back on themselves, and lonesome, for all their superficial comradeship. But that gray hopelessness to which they were resigned without being able to accept it—that was the unbearable part. The monotony, the everlasting boredom—I had already had my fill of that.

8

UNTIL now I had only been in Vladimir's section and in the mechanized part of the mine. The chief engineer asked me almost daily where I wanted to go next. Apparently he still hoped to please me by showing me many interesting aspects of the mine. But for the time being I chose Vladimir's section. He and I got along very well. In the eyes of the workers he was the most sympathetic of all the foremen.

It struck me that becoming a foreman was quite a problem, and several foremen talked openly about it to me. In Filondange it was the custom to give that position to experienced workers who had worked especially well in the mine for a considerable time. But very often an odd change of outlook took place in the men who were promoted. The appointment, together with the official recognition of merit that it implied, as well as the fact that a foreman is in charge of fifty men, brought with it a strong feeling of superiority. The new foremen became "important." They would often shout commands in a dictatorial manner. Conscious of having arrived, many a foreman isolated himself from the workers—and when he didn't, the workers themselves isolated him, even if he still belonged to their own circle. Perhaps just because of it: they weren't going to take any nonsense from one of their own kind. The young foremen who came from the mining school and had never been ordinary laborers—apart from their apprenticeship—went over much better. In general they were jovial and congenial fellows who didn't care much about their "dignity." They lacked authority, however, with the older and more experienced workers. It could happen that they issued orders against the better judgment of the veteran miners. Besides, those young foremen—often under thirty years of age—did not have the robust strength of seasoned workers. Often they were physically unable to show what they wanted done. And it takes physical strength to command respect in the mine.

Vladimir did not come from the mining school; he was just a good, hard worker. But he had become the protégé of the chief engineer because he was an excellent football player as well. The workers know very well that this is often the way to better jobs, and usually they are fiercely resentful of it. But they couldn't help liking Vladimir in spite of the reason for his promotion. He had remained an "ordinary" worker with heart and soul.

After some time I went to another part of the mine with a foreman who was not taken seriously by either his colleagues or the workers. His name was Mora; he was of South American origin. He was a self-educated man who had acquired a great knowledge of geology and was continually showing it off. He told me that there was a lot of jealousy among the foremen and that they resented the fact that he tried to explain the secrets of the mine to the workers. He didn't fit into the businesslike relationship that exists among the mine workers. On my first tour through his section I had to listen to endless explanations (of which, to tell the truth, I understood little) about the origin of iron ore, about the different geological eras, about chemical reactions, etc. But he also talked about things that did interest me.

His section extended a long way and had many abandoned, silent corridors where hardly anyone ever set foot. Rocks rose up around us in weird and menacing shapes. The lamps on our helmets shone like searchlights in the darkness of this underworld. Mora also carried a carbide lamp, which threw a much brighter light on the brown soil and on our legs. The abandoned corridors were wider and higher than those in Vladimir's section, but Mora could still reach the ceiling with his stick—a matter of the greatest importance. The first thing the miners did in the morning was check the ceiling in their section. They tapped against it with an iron rod, and when a rock made a suspicious sound they pried it loose. It was hard work sometimes, but no one started work until it had been done. The foremen always tapped the corridors in use on their first checking round. No matter how massive the layers of rock seem, they are always changing inside. Where we walked it was very dangerous, for nobody had checked these passages for a long time. With an experienced eye Mora watched sharply.

Crrrack . . . boom! . . . there was a terrific roar in one of the side corridors. My heart began beating rapidly.

"Something is falling down," Mora said by way of explanation.

"It sure is!"

"The mine is about eight miles long and eight miles wide. The parts that have been exhausted usually close up by themselves."

The motionless mass around us seemed to be ready to demonstrate this process at any minute. Man is but an ant in creation. All he can do is put his hands over his head, and that doesn't stop a few thousand tons of rock from falling.

We turned into a smaller corridor.

"It's a little more dangerous here. Walk behind me along the wall."

The bottom inclined slowly toward the ceiling, of which entire layers had weakened and torn loose, ready to cave in at any moment.

"You see, this corridor used to be shored up, but the support was taken away long ago. Now you would expect the ceiling to fall any time. And it will, of course, but meanwhile the weight above presses through the walls and pushes up the floor. That's why this corridor goes up toward the ceiling."

We had reached the end. There was a small hole between ceiling and floor through which we could just manage to crawl. From there we jumped down into a corridor where there was no danger.

In one part miners were busy drilling and loading. The ceiling was a mixture of gray and brown rock.

Mora pointed upward with his stick.

"The gray you see covers up the first layer of ore. It dates from the snake era."

In vain I searched my memory to place that particular era.

"You see, here you have a petrified snake."

Indeed, a coiled snake was clearly visible.

"Here's another one, and there another one."

There were about ten of them together.

A small piece of rock lay in front of us. It was broken up, white as snow inside, but not solid all the way through. The shape of a lower jaw with the marks of snake teeth could clearly be distinguished. Another piece of rock bore the shape of a snake on the outside.

"If you would break that piece you'd see that the whole snake was petrified, skin and all."

We broke it. Inside it was white with blue veins—all of stone.

The workers didn't pay the slightest attention to the story. It apparently didn't make the least difference to them whether we saw petrified snakes or petrified rabbits. Rock to them was rock.

We continued our walk through prehistoric times, and after a while Mora kicked against a block of basalt.

"Does this mean anything to you?" he asked.

"No."

"This is the end of the mine."

"Why do they mark it with a stone? You can't go on anyway!"

"No, but this stone was worn away by the sea. The sea used to reach to here. So there's no possibility of finding ore any farther on. And here you have shells!" He pointed to another part of the ceiling.

There they were, indeed.

The next day I had to work as a hauler. There were three of us.
The hewer was a Pole. The man I was supposed to help was a
North African from Algiers. We had a beautiful *chantier*, wide
and spacious. We started, as always, by testing the ceiling. Then
the real work began: the Pole did the drilling and we did the
loading. The African was about twenty-five years old, and spoke
French very well. He had a beautiful head, jet-black hair, and
mysteriously sparkling eyes; he smiled warmly whenever we had
to push away our two-and-a-half tons. His voice was as warm and
dark as his face.

The North Africans I had met until then seemed to me people
with a warm heart, passionate and also fanatical. In general they
did not seek contact with the French.

The two of us ate together. Whether I had been nicer to him
during work than the other miners I don't know, but he talked as
if I were his best friend.

"You live in the barracks?" he asked.

"Yes."

"Are you home this afternoon?"

"Why? Do you want to come and see me?"

He smiled with the shyness I had noticed before in young
Africans.

"Yes."

How had I deserved this?

"I'd like to ask you many things."

"Good!"

"I was with a girl yesterday!"

"Were you? Where?"

"In Filondange."

"In her home?"

"Yes. You're Dutch, aren't you?"

"Yes."

"I had parked my bicycle in front of the house, and when I
came out it was gone."

"Gone?"

"Yes, and when I came home it was standing in front of my house!"

I thought of the magic of the Far East.

"And do you know who did it?" he went on.

"No."

"Her fiancé. He spied on me from the bushes."

His eyes sparkled fire.

"If I ever run into him, you know what's going to happen to him?"

"No."

He made a throat-slitting gesture.

I looked at him. Was that what we were going to talk about in the afternoon? The North Africans were quick with the knife, and he would not be the first to send someone to eternity.

We loaded blocks of ore into the cart until it was time to quit. With the smile of an accomplice he attached his lamp to the edge of the cart each time, and like blood brothers we pushed the load together. We managed to fill seventeen carts, which came to more than forty tons.

But he didn't murder anyone.

He had to go to the surface with the train of oxygen bottles; I stayed behind with Mora and a group of workers.

"Did you work well this morning?" he inquired.

"Yes."

"You didn't quarrel with the Islamite?"

"Oh, no!"

"Islam, Islam?" asked an old Italian who had seen us working together. "Is that African a Mohammedan?"

"Of course he is, they all are!" Mora laughed. The old man looked so upset that the other workers began to laugh, too.

"Mohammedans?" The Italian probably thought they were the same as cannibals.

"What's the matter with you?" said Mora. "Islam is a religion like all the others. All religions are good!"

In Mora's section there was a long, narrow, dead-end corridor.

There was drilling and loading going on at the end of it, but the ventilation didn't reach that far. When the four of us arrived there in the morning it was just as cool as in the rest of the mine, but somewhat stuffier. You could almost taste the lack of oxygen.

Less than fifteen minutes later perspiration was pouring from our bodies. We had to take our shirts off.

From the beginning the loading went slowly. After the first blasting we worked in dust and smoke till the end. The heat was stifling, and it did not let up.

My three co-workers were Frenchmen. During lunch they remarked calmly and slowly that it was suicide to work there.

Silicosis, the ghost of the mine! In the iron mines it occurs much more frequently than in the coal mines. Only recently has silicosis come to be considered an occupational hazard. It had taken a long time for this to be accepted, my co-workers told me. It happened too often and would cost the insurance companies too much money.

The four of us didn't manage more than four dump-carts. My friends didn't have much pep; they just couldn't be bothered. They would get extra money above their minimum wage anyway, because of working conditions.

Almost every day I saw Erich and Hans with his friends. Hans was talking about the fair that was coming Sunday and Monday.

"I can't go," I said.

"What do you mean, you can't go?"

"I have to go to Strasbourg about my passport."

"You can go another day!"

"When? I'm on the morning shift the whole week. The consulate is closed on Sundays. If I go Saturday afternoon after work, or maybe Sunday afternoon, I can be back by Monday night. I can't get to Strasbourg and back in one afternoon, it's impossible. Besides, I have to attend to some business there."

"I think," said Max, "that Strasbourg is more interesting than the fair."

I heard Mass in the cathedral, and I listened to the organ playing. The enormous church was full; there are still churches in
France that are not empty on Sundays.

The next Sunday I went to hear Mass in Filondange. The
church stood between the village and the mine colony. Among
the few miners there I recognized Erich; the rest were villagers.
The colony had its own little church, which belonged to the mine,
but not many miners went there, either.

One day I was cycling from the mine to the barracks with
Erich when he asked me: "Do you know what's the worst thing
about life here?"

"No."

"The loneliness and the boredom. Everyone lives for himself.
The only one I can talk to is you. I haven't got any other friends.
At least no one I have anything in common with."

"What about Hans and the others?"

"That's quite different. I don't know how to express it."

He was a nice fellow, liked by everyone.

9

M. Piron stopped me as I was leaving the mine and invited me
to dinner that evening. I arrived at his home around seven.

We talked about the housing situation, of which he was in
charge. It was a very great problem. There was not enough space,
people had to live too close together and suffered all the conse-
quences of overcrowding. We also talked about wages. The
hewers and haulers were the best off. Apart from the minimum

wage, they got an extra bonus according to the tonnage they produced. The wages of the underground workers fell into six categories and ranged from about 800 francs to about 1,100 francs a day. But a hewer with a minimum wage of 1,100 francs could, if he worked hard, bring it up to 2,000, 2,500 and even 3,000 francs a day, and that was not bad. On the other hand the men who were in charge of the maintenance of the mine never got more than about 1,000 francs. They and the above-ground workers were the worst off, and had a hard time making ends meet. These people had a more or less fixed wage, with a little extra once in a while. Their wages fell into seven categories and ranged from 720 to 1,000 francs a day. Even with an extra allowance for children, life was very difficult for them.

"But there isn't any real misery, you'll have to admit that!" M. Piron said.

"As far as wages are concerned, that's true."

"Besides, wages increase according to the years of service, but that doesn't really amount to much."

"And insurance?"

"That's deducted, of course."

I looked at my first wage slip. I didn't yet have the right to a hauler's wage because I came under category 2.

Days: 9
Hours of work: 72
Hourly wage: 95.34 frs.
Total amount: 6,864 frs.
Compensation: 619 frs. (This was a permanent addition to the wage.)
Extra allowance: 617 frs.
Gross wage: 8,100 frs.
Heating allowance: 263 frs.
Net wage: 8,363 frs.

But then came insurance, storeroom expenses, etc., and my wages shrank from 8,363 francs to 8,100, to 7,513, to 7,301, to 6,653, to 4,753 and finally to the 4,613 francs which was actually paid to me. Considering my special case, I couldn't object, and I lived in the barracks, which cost me only about 2,500 francs for nine days, so that I had a little over 2,000 francs left for myself.

But suppose I were married and didn't live in the barracks, then I would get an extra allowance of 20% of my wage for each of the first two children, and 50% for three children. Suppose I should get 12,000 francs in nine days for a family with three children—that is 1,400 francs a day. We could manage, perhaps, but only with difficulty.

"Yes, but your house wouldn't cost you anything, you'd have free light and water and a piece of ground to cultivate!"

"And finally I might reach the sixth category," I said, "then things would get easier."

"Yes, except if you worked above ground, then your wage would remain about the same."

The engineer insisted that I come for dinner one evening. He had a big villa with a tennis court next to it. Dogs began barking wildly when I tried to open the gate. He came out and told me to wait until he was with me, for otherwise the dogs were dangerous. Inside it was very elegant, and in my plain gray trousers and khaki jacket I didn't fit in with the surroundings at all. The wife of the engineer was a most charming lady who had a strong resemblance to the wife of France's president. In aristocratic fashion we sat on elegant chairs in the drawing room at a great distance from one another, as coffee was brought in on a serving cart. The children were allowed to introduce themselves formally and then had to withdraw; only the eldest daughter could stay. I couldn't understand why I had been invited, for the conversation was nothing but small talk. It was painful from beginning to end, because I couldn't make out what his attitude towards me was. I noticed that he was very much interested in my reason for working in the mine. He made it apparent that he didn't know, but thought he ought to know; yet he couldn't ask me directly since he had to pretend that he did know. And when I didn't confide in him spontaneously he started hinting, which obviously annoyed his wife. He asked my opinion about many different things. He let me talk, watched me with a mechanical smile and said "yes" in a way that made me ask: "Don't you agree?", whereupon he would come back with "Oh yes, you are absolutely right!" He wasn't committing himself and I wasn't, either, and we both knew it.

When he was called away for a few minutes, his wife asked me how I liked life in the colony.

"My personal experience isn't so important, but for those people life is so gray and monotonous that it's spiritually and culturally deadening."

"Oh, now you say exactly what I think, too. I really pity those people. But my husband always says: 'Why do you get so excited?' I come from Paris, and my father was a professor; we had an intellectually stimulating milieu. But here! We still have a car and can go places, but these people can't ever get away!" She was serious and a little sad.

The engineer returned.

"Tell me, how are things in the barracks?"

He was in charge of the barracks.

"Well, I don't need to tell you what it looks like."

"No, but how is the food, for instance?"

"It's good enough for me, but . . . ."

"Don't hesitate. I put a man in charge there and I have only to snap my fingers and he's kicked out. I like drastic action!"

As if that were the solution!

"It's not bad, but a little monotonous," I continued.

"Are there any essential things lacking?"

"That depends on what you call essential. For instance, we eat the meat with our fingers. It's possible, if you try!"

"Haha," he laughed, "I understand! There were knives once, but they have gradually disappeared." He noted down: "Knives."

"What else?"

"There isn't the slightest bit of comfort."

"Well, what would you want?"

"A table and a few chairs in each room."

"Come now, is that really necessary? Besides, there's no room."

"Exactly. A little more space would also be very pleasant."

"Those guys are not in the barracks for fun."

"I think it's important that they should at least feel at home!"

"So you want easy chairs?" he said sarcastically.

"That wouldn't be such a bad idea."

"Hah! And what else?"

"Better service!"

"First- or second-class hotel?"

"I mean mainly that the meals are served too much as the army does it."

"You mean the self-service system?"

"If you can call standing in line with a plate in your hand self-service!"

"But that's the system in American cafeterias!"

"The principle is the same, but the practice is different. I have eaten more than once in American cafeterias, and it was quite different."

"These men don't have so many pretensions!"

"It's true they don't criticize very much!"

"And if they do, they can leave. What else?"

"In the morning there's no water for washing."

"They probably wouldn't wash even if they could. Besides, it's difficult to change the arrangement. Half the day Marondange receives water from the mine, and Filondange the other half. There is a project under way for an inter-community water supply, but they're not making much headway."

"The result is that the toilets are a filthy mess."

"There is someone assigned to keep the house and the toilets clean. I was in the barracks not long ago, and it looked tidy."

"Probably because you were coming. Besides, one man in charge can't improve the situation: three toilets for fifty or more men!"

Dinner was announced.

The one thing written down on his slip of paper was "Knives." The only improvement that could actually be made!

We sat down to dinner.

"Do you play tennis?" the engineer asked.

"Yes, but not too well."

"Pierre, tomorrow morning you two play a game together."

Pierre, in the fourth year of high school, nodded.

"I can't, I have to work tomorrow morning," I remarked.

"I'll give you a day off. You come and play a few games at six in the morning; later it is much too hot. I'll come myself, too. After that you can go to the mine and look at the activities above ground. You haven't seen those yet. Your salary will continue."

I didn't feel at all like it, but couldn't refuse.

During the meal, too, behavior was very upper-class.

"What do you think of my son Pierre?"

I smiled a little.

"An unmanageable boy, but since he's been studying with the Marist Fathers, he has changed completely. We ourselves couldn't do a thing with him. I must say I respect them for managing it. I take my hat off to them." He made an accompanying gesture. "If I had two, I'd take off both of them."

Late at night I cycled back. I would have a thousand times preferred to stay in the barracks. I passed the mine with its lamps arching high over the railroad yard. Men were shouting to each other. Dump-carts clattered toward the cupola. Cars were loaded and locomotives rattled. Clouds of steam were drifting from the light into the darkness.

"Hey, you've got no light!"

That was nothing new. I turned off without answering. A strange, uneasy feeling had taken possession of me.

The part of the mine that was above ground was not exactly beautiful: a factory-like complex of buildings. Ceaselessly dump-carts were drawn upward on a cable to the cupola, a distance of about thirty-five yards. There the loads were weighed and noted down according to the numbers chalked on the carts. I stood watching it. I knew the story of these carts. Get an empty one, keep loading it till you dropped, then push it with your head and arms, or with your hips, using all the strength in your body. Here they came triumphantly above ground, loaded with ore that had never yet seen daylight.

The ore was dumped into a big hopper. Underneath, railroad cars were filled with it by opening a sliding gate. Fifteen dump-carts were about enough to load one railroad car—the work of three men for one shift. Forty tons—how much would that bring in? the workers wonder. They may get 3,000 francs per man for it, 9,000 francs altogether (about $25.—). What happens to the rest of the money? It is used for the upkeep of the mine, for buying equipment, paying personnel, for building a colony. And is there nothing left after that? They don't believe so. How else would the capitalists get their cars, their houses, their possessions, their wealth? The mass exists so that the few can live well. That's how they see it, and they say, "It's not fair."

On the dump-carts rolled; long trains filled up and transported the precious raw material to the blast furnaces of the Saar. To make guns, the men say sarcastically.

When I got on my bicycle a priest passed the gate of the mine. With a deep bow he took off his hat and swept it all the way to his knees. A little later he passed another miner. Again he bowed and took off his hat. Well meant, no doubt, but a little dramatic.

"The director asks if you would come and see him tonight," M. Piron told me one day as I was leaving the mine. Had the director forgotten that I'd rather have no contact with him during the time I worked in the mine? Or was there a special reason?

"What time is he expecting me?"

"About seven o'clock."

"Where?"

"In his villa."

At seven o'clock I rang the bell. The director himself opened the door and shook hands with me.

"Let's go and sit in the garden. My wife and children are vacationing in the Vosges, so I am all by myself. I'd like to have a talk with you."

We sat down in a little arbor.

"Well, what about your impressions?" he began.

"I've got plenty of impressions, but they're not all digested yet. First I'd like to see what conditions are like in other mines."

"Our people aren't bad, are they?"

"Oh no, on the contrary, very friendly."

"And they have no reason to complain. They have their homes, their pieces of land, and they earn enough to make ends meet."

"A good percentage of them, at least," I said. "But there are others who have a hard time. Yet I admit I haven't come across any extreme poverty. I think the workers here have problems of a different nature."

"Not that wages aren't a problem," he observed. "There are people here who never earn enough, who say they can't live on their wages, while others in exactly the same circumstances can live reasonably well. If you can tell me what a fair wage is, you know more than I do."

"I don't think wages are the real source of dissatisfaction."

"You mean to say they're dissatisfied?"

"What I mean is that they are resigned to their fate. This is the way things are, they think, and this is the way they'll probably always be."

"What do you mean by that?"

"Everything."

"You speak in riddles."

"Well," I tried to explain, "the whole life of the workers is a source of discontent. They themselves couldn't tell what the exact reason is. That's why they pick out the most obvious and the most simple thing—their wages—if they can't live on them, that is. If they can, they pretend to be satisfied, but they aren't

really. That's clear from a lot of things. Or they express dissatisfaction with other aspects of their lives, to which the wage-
conscious group is resigned as to an unalterable fate."

"Fate, fate—what fate are you talking about?" he asked im-
patiently.

"A complex of things, hard to define, but all interrelated."

"Hm."

"Take a few examples at random: how do these people live?
One might say they live well, for the roofs and the walls of their
homes are solid. I haven't come across hovels in the strict sense
of the word. But the houses are depressing and monotonous. This
doesn't make for conditions of real distress, but it helps to mark
the workers as an anonymous mass. One can tell that a man is
'only a worker' by the way he lives."

"What can I do about it? Those houses were built forty, fifty
years ago."

"I don't say it is your fault. Neither is it a condition prevalent
only at this mine. You can find the same thing almost everywhere.
I only mention it as an example of what depresses the workers."

"But we have realized that ourselves. You'll agree with me that
the new houses are totally different."

"I certainly do; they're practically ideal!"

"Please go on."

"Take for instance the main street of the colony. The houses
along there badly need a new paint job, and the street itself has
no sidewalk. You couldn't call it a slum, but it's uncared-for, and
it's another thing that marks the workers' world."

"Come now, people really don't raise a fuss about that."

"But it is one of the elements in their general attitude of 'That's
the way things are.' They won't strike because of it, but they say:
'Nothing much, that street of ours, is it?'"

"Don't get the idea that *I'm* so enthusiastic about the colony!"
he objected.

"You have to understand me, too," I went on. "You want to
know what is so depressing about the workers' world. All the

things I've mentioned are secondary, and none of them causes emergency conditions. Now take the barracks. A place to eat and sleep, and that's all. The food is sufficient, and you can sleep well enough. But it isn't a home! There isn't even a minimum of comfort. As for recreation, the only thing is a bowling alley behind the house. When the boys want to play football they have to cycle back to the mine. No one does that who just wants to play for a little fun. So all they can do is sit around on the steps or drink away their boredom in a bar. It's mentally deadening. It's in the barracks, if anywhere, that you realize you're 'only a worker'."

"I told you in the beginning that it wouldn't be so easy."

"It doesn't make too much difference to me personally. After all, I'll only work here for a short time, but if you have to live here for many years, you can't help ending up by just vegetating."

"Well, yes . . . ."

"And these are only a few of the material aspects that influence the mentality of the workers. Wages don't really play that big a part. No matter how well-paid the workers are, the depression remains. There is practically no cultural life."

"What do you want? The mine can't take care of everything. Let me start by telling you that I'd like to do everything possible for the workers. But preferably not as director of the mine. That would put me in an awkward position. There is a tendency on the part of industry nowadays to take complete charge of the life of the workers. The industry has to provide the worker with a milieu which offers him everything. We almost end up cooking their meals for them. That would be the other extreme, which I'm sure the workers don't want either. You may know the case of Michelin. Michelin shoes, Michelin socks, Michelin shirts, Michelin here, Michelin there, Michelin everywhere. He dominated the life of the workers to such an extent that they went on strike against him. This kind of paternalism is against my convictions. That doesn't mean that I don't want to do anything for the workers. Today industry is required to be responsible for social welfare. I can't escape that, and I don't want to, either. But it goes against the grain when the director of a mine has to get involved with the private lives of the miners. I consider freedom and independence man's noblest possessions and I would be infringing their rights if I arranged their lives for them. The workers have to create their own lives and their own surroundings. We must not increase their dependence. More and more they assume the attitude that things are to be done for them. They think they gain that way. But the opposite is true. What they lose in independence, they lose in human dignity, too. If people condemn a system where the state is all-powerful, why don't they condemn this kind of paternalism? Or is the only fault of state supremacy that it affects freedom of thought?" He looked at me and waited for a reply.

"If an industry takes care of the workers off the job, it isn't necessarily paternalism," I said. "The industry doesn't use only the physical strength of the worker, it uses his spiritual strength as well. It's impossible to separate the two, except in abstract reasoning. Along with the wages, the industry gives its people the ability to live physically: to eat, to sleep, to dress. Perhaps you would add: 'and to live and develop culturally and spiritually.' But is this true? Usually the salary isn't sufficient for that, and even if it were, we would still have to cope with the fact that the cultural life of these people is so weak that it cannot develop by itself. In any case the slightest initiative that comes from the workers' world has to be felt and encouraged. By whom? By the industry, it seems to me. The realization of initiative usually costs money. If the wages aren't high enough for that, something is probably wrong with the wages. I think that the industry could at least help out. It doesn't have to do everything, and whatever it does contribute can be in the form of voluntary co-operation with the workers. In my opinion industry must often take the initiative to help develop the workers culturally. Why couldn't this be done in consultation with them? That way nobody's dignity would suffer."

"Why should industry have to take such initiative? Isn't that overstepping the boundaries of its function?"

"If you see an industry as something purely economic, perhaps. But I wonder if an industry exists only for producing goods, and also whether the economy is concerned only with the problems of supply and demand. A mine is more than just iron ore that has to be marketed. There is always a human factor, without which a mine couldn't exist. The mine functions because of people, who cannot be regarded merely as 'labor' without ignoring reality. Man as 'beast of burden' is nothing but an abstraction. It seems to me that the industry is responsible for the worker as a whole person, not just during working hours, but also when he is off duty—though not in a paternal way, for that would go against his nature, as you pointed out yourself."

"Responsible for the worker outside his work? You are an exponent of a modern tendency. The other day a priest from one of the villages around here came to visit me. He, too, talked about the responsibilities of industry toward its workers. He came all the way just to talk about that. I didn't agree with him in the slightest, not to mention that I think these things are none of his business.

"My predecessor built a church here. But what does that mean, a church belonging to the mine? Is a mine Catholic? The present priest wants money to improve the interior. He wants draperies and things. One day they may go so far as to ask for easy chairs for the church so they can attract people with comfort. Now we have a beautiful church here, paid for and kept up by the mine, but hardly anyone uses it. The mine gives the workers free homes, free light and water, a piece of land to cultivate, and wages too. There are limits to what it can afford, if it wants to stay in business."

"Of course there are limits, but we're talking about the principle of industry's being responsible for the workers."

"To a certain extent it is. That's generally accepted," he admitted.

"Yes, but to what extent? That depends on a correct analysis
of reality. Take a colony like this one. It is a community of people,
united by their work and by belonging to the same class. United,
in fact, by the mine. The mine created the community. But apart
from that limited feeling of belonging, people here live rather
isolated from one another. They are people without a common
culture. They come from many countries and each goes his own
way. There is no common ground, unless it is that of a depressing
monotony and boredom. I believe that the mine should help build
more human, more cultural surroundings, for it has brought this
colony into being and is responsible for it. It has created conditions in which no human being could exist without being dissatisfied. At the same time it has created susceptibility to Communist
propaganda. But I agree with you that the independence of the
workers must be respected. It is hard to say, though, what exactly
should be done."

"I agree with you there," he said.

"I think one should start with the cultural development of the
young people. Then, in the long run, initiative may come from
the workers themselves."

He got up.

"Let's take a walk through the garden."

The garden was large, with many fruit trees. He picked different kinds of fruit as we walked along, and handed them to me.
He was serious but friendly.

"Believe me, the fate of my workers does concern me. But it
covers so much ground."

"Yes."

"And I myself am dependent on the world market, on the prevailing economy."

"True . . . ."

"And on the way in which industry has been regarded in the
past."

"Meanwhile human nature avenges itself. Human values in
labor have been so neglected."

"You can't change these things overnight."

We went inside and sat in the drawing room.

"What would you like? Cognac, wine, liqueur? I can recommend the Chartreuse."

He poured the Chartreuse.

"Do you smoke?"

"Yes, please."

He put various boxes on the table.

"Cigarettes? Cigars? Being Dutch, you smoke cigars of course."

"I haven't smoked one for a long time."

"These are very good."

He offered me a Havana.

"Talking about labor, what do you think of the underground work?"

"I know it's hard!"

"Yes, but you need an hour to get started and another hour to get back; six working hours is reasonable, even if the work is heavy."

"It's not the hours, but . . . !"

"Go on!"

"The men work as a 'labor force,' not as human beings, except perhaps in the mechanized part of the mine. They work for money and nothing else. The meaning of work escapes most people. They are forced to work because they have to live. Work is not considered a part of life—or rather it is regarded as a part of life we have to put up with. And it deadens them."

"How do you mean?"

"They are not appreciated as human beings. The facilities above ground are colorless and inadequate. It's a question of economy. They have to wait out in the open until the mine train leaves, regardless of weather. Why can't the worker be treated with respect as a human being, even where he works?"

"I am aware of that, but this is our inheritance. I didn't build the mine, nor the colony."

"All right, but meanwhile the morale of the workers is affected, and that's what we are talking about. They are transported like sardines in a can. They are supposed to put up with that, as with everything else. But all the same. . . . The main galleries are badly lighted, the side corridors not at all. They just have to make do with their lamps. The ventilation is often insufficient. But people have to work, and they do it to earn as much money as possible. Nobody takes the actual human effort into account, only the results. The workers know this very well: they exist only to produce. The management pays them, and that's all. Worn out, they come back to an environment that offers them nothing. Why economize at the expense of the worker? Is industry nothing but an economic institution?

"There is a great deal of the joy of life in work. The men express themselves in their strength. They are proud of it and they enjoy it. But this joy comes to a dead end if it doesn't lead to an appreciation of the community as a whole. The working class is almost a caste—fortunately they are emancipating themselves— and the individual worker is thrown back almost entirely on himself. Why can't their work be called to public attention, the way sports results are? After all, society depends on them. If the workers find they are appreciated, for instance, on radio, in movies and in the press, if they see that improvements in working conditions are not made solely for the sake of higher production, if they get a decent wage and can enjoy a little culture, they will know that they belong to society as human beings, and not just as a labor force.

"The elements that hold down the workers are manifold and interdependent, but you probably know that better than I do. I am only giving you my impressions, since you ask for them. I don't think higher wages alone would help, for that is not the core of the problem; neither is social welfare. The questions are: What is the general attitude toward industry? What function does the worker as a human being have in it? What is the function of industry and its workers in society? What, if anything, is being done about it?

"One might call the workers' mentality an inferiority complex.

But this is only a sign that something is wrong somewhere, which in turn creates symptoms like revolutions and strikes—to mention only the more alarming ones.

"I don't know whether I'm right, but this is the way I see it. Anyway, I didn't come here to study social problems."

"Are you making headway with your own research?" he asked.

"I think most people still have faith, even if they don't practise religion."

"I think so, too," he agreed.

"Social order and religion are inter-related, anyway. I see the latent social revolution as a return to the primary values of life and society, coupled necessarily with a return to the primary values of religion. People don't want façades any longer. I don't see the apparent indifference and even resistance to the Church as something purely negative. It is at the same time a condemnation of the rigidity of the Church and a desire for a more authentic Christian experience. People are open to anything that is genuine and true. A priest could limit himself to explaining the meaning of existence and the importance of the Revelation and the Church in people's lives. But there is a barrier between the clergy and the people."

"I'm not a believer myself, as you may know," the director said seriously, and continued: "But I think the main task of the Church is to preach and to practise love. That is what I believe people expect of it."

"I believe, too," I replied, "that the work of the priest should not become mainly sociological. Priests cannot bring about effective social solutions. They are social enough when they show people their Christian obligations. The thing is to make people realize that everything in life has meaning. One should be able to be a Christian even in the greatest misery — which doesn't mean that people should be expected to put up with injustice, unless they have attained a considerable degree of holiness. It's a question of the joy of Christianity under all circumstances. This joy is missing. People need it, but they have to be taught realistically how to acquire it. Through the human contact which friendship creates, a worker priest could do much good in this respect. It might even be the most effective way to bridge the gap between clergy and people."

"As far as that's concerned," remarked the director, "I often don't understand the behavior of the higher clergy. We asked the Bishop for a priest just for the mine, because it is a community in itself with its own atmosphere and its own problems. You say yourself that a worker-priest could do much good here. But the Bishop won't send us a priest because that would interfere with the proper functioning of the existing parishes. The result is that nothing is achieved at all. The parish is doing very poorly, and the workers remain alienated from the Church."

It was after eleven when I cycled back to the barracks. I hurried to be in time to eat with the latecomers from the afternoon shift.

Mora counted on my coming to visit him. He wanted to show me a big collection of special stones. I went one evening, and while we were sitting in the kitchen the priest came to give Holy Communion to his father. Mora asked me to amuse myself for a little while, and left to be present at the giving of the sacrament. I thought of the incident with my Algerian friend not long ago, when the old Italian miner had been so upset at the thought of Islam. And I reflected that Mora had never told me whether among all the religions that were, according to him, equally good, there might be some that were better than others.

I was sitting in Hans', Klaus' and Max's room. It was Sunday afternoon and we were going to a movie in town.

"We'd better changes clothes," said Klaus.

"Why?" I protested. "You look all right as you are, and I don't have anything else."

But they were already getting out other clothes.

"Put on a suit of mine," Max offered.

"No, I'm going like this."

"Come on, which do you want, the blue one or the brown one?"

"That's some wardrobe you have. What are you wearing yourself?"

"I'm going to wear that one."

"I'm going as I am," I insisted.

"Shut up. Here's a suit, here's a shirt, here's a tie. Or do you want another one? Come on, put it on."

"What's the matter with you all? Can't I go like this?" I was wearing my ordinary khaki jacket.

"It's your own business!"

"Dammit, it's raining," Hans said, struggling with his tie.

"Then I'll have to stay home. I don't have a coat." I had left it somewhere in the colony.

"Are you crazy? Take one of mine," Max offered again.

"Hey, what kind of a guy are you? How many suits and coats do you have?"

He laughed.

"Dammit, now I have to wear that damn coat of mine," Hans grumbled. "Give me one of yours, too, Max."

Max handed them out. A coat for Hans. A coat for me. Two raincoats, almost brand new. He put his suits back in the closet.

"Capitalist!"

He laughed and said nothing.

10

THE end of my stay in Filondange was approaching. I had to go and see the priest of the mine's church. I had made his acquaintance at M. Piron's and told him that I was a priest, too.

He had asked me to come and see him, and I went just before I left. He was surrounded by children, and busy putting candy in bags for the coming fair. A simple man with a good heart. His parents were living with him. The clergy in Alsace-Lorraine is not as impoverished as in the rest of France, because Lorraine still has German laws and the clergy there is state-subsidized. Otherwise Alsace-Lorraine has become completely French. The children don't even speak German any more.

I had dinner at the priest's.

"What proportion of your parish is practising?" I asked him.

"If I say ten per cent, I exaggerate. The workers practise least of all."

"Do you have much contact with them?"

"There is no group life of any kind," he said sadly. "I don't know how I could get people together. They are friendly enough, but it never goes beyond a little chat. I went to the casino a few times, but that's a hopeless business."

"Why?"

"Well, when I go I have to drink. Somebody offers me something. If I refuse, he thinks I don't like him. Then another offers me a drink. I can't refuse him, because I accepted it from the first one. I just can't keep up with that. And I don't get anywhere with it, anyway."

"Do people still have their children baptized?"

"Oh yes, all of them."

"And the last sacraments?"

"At the last moment, just before it is too late."

"Yet a lot could be done with these people," I said. "Do you know the boys from the barracks?"

"No. Your barracks don't belong to my parish."

"Spiritually, they are left to their fate."

"You could also say that they leave themselves to their fate. They simply won't be approached."

"Yet they are open to anything that really touches their lives."

Marcel was lying on the street beside his house, fixing a car.

"What do you think of my car?"

"Is it yours?"

"Yes, I bought it second-hand, but it's in good condition."

"Capitalist!"

He laughed. "We're taking a vacation in it, Lucien and his wife, and my wife and I."

"When?"

"As soon as possible. The damn thing is that I never know when I can leave. If I apply for a certain day and they approve, they may tell me the evening before that I can't go. That's happened before."

Lucien joined us. He tapped me on the shoulder: "How's life?"

"Okay."

"We're going on a trip, as you see."

"Yes, wonderful. I'm leaving, too."

"You're leaving?" Marcel asked. He got up from the street. "For good?"

"Yes."

"You don't say! When?"

"Tuesday."

"Why?"

"I want to work in a different kind of mine."

"Well, I'm damned. Where are you going?"

"I don't know yet."

"You don't know yet? Why don't you stay a while? I'm really sorry you're leaving. We got along so well."

"As far as that goes, I'm sorry too."

"Come and have dinner with us before you go. How about Sunday night?"

"Fine."

On Sunday night Lucien was there, too.

"Where are you going Tuesday?"

"To town. Then I'll decide what to do."

"And we won't see you again?"

"I don't know. I guess it'll be difficult."

"If you're ever in the neighborhood, drop in. You can stay for a few days and sleep on the couch. Then we can have another of our evenings and talk about music, about life, and about religion. You'll write, won't you?"

"Sure."

"If you find work not too far from here, we might come and see you by car. What time are you leaving Tuesday?"

"About four."

"We'll take you to town! We'll come and get you at the barracks."

I sat in the room with Hans, Klaus and Max.

"I'm leaving," I said suddenly.

"You're kidding."

"No, I'm really leaving."

"That's not fair, dammit! Where are you going?"

"I don't know yet. To a different kind of mine."

For a moment Hans fumed like a chimney. He grabbed me: "You can't do that!"

"I can, too."

He sat down and looked at me, his head in his fists.

"I want to see a different kind of mine. I told you in the beginning that I wouldn't stay long."

"You can leave . . . but what about us?"

He couldn't have reminded me more painfully that I was not a worker.

"When are you going?"

"Tuesday afternoon."

"You'll write, won't you?"

"Sure."

He got an idea and recovered his good humor.

"Hey, we'll come to see you!"

"Where?"

"Wherever you are. All the iron mines are around here. You won't be more than forty miles away at most."

"Maybe we could meet in Metz."

"That's even better. You write and we'll meet you."

"It's a date."

"We'll see you off Tuesday, of course."

"Where to?"

"To town. We'll have a last drink together."

"Okay, but Marcel and Lucien are seeing me off, too."

"Who are they?"

"Marcel? He is the technician of the Joy."

"Dammit, you know everybody."

"Many people around here know him."

"A technician?" Klaus asked. He had studied at a technical school.

"It may be interesting for you to meet him. A nice guy." I said.

"Yes, not a bad idea."

"They're coming to get me by car. In style!"

"By car?"

"Yes, he has a second-hand car."

"How many can get into it?"

"Four. Maybe five, with a little goodwill."

"Then I'll go by bus," Max said.

The engineer stopped me.

"You're leaving Tuesday afternoon?"

"Yes."

"Come and have lunch with me for the last time on Tuesday."

"With pleasure. What time shall I come?"

"About noon."

In the morning I took leave of the director.

"Do you know yet what mine you're going to?"

"No, not yet. I'll find out in Metz what the possibilities are."

"If you like, I can call a colleague of mine and arrange things right away. Do you have any preference?"

"I'd like a mine different from this one, so I can compare."

"St. Germain? Very different people and a very different mine?"

"That sounds all right."

He put through a call. The director wasn't in.

"You're leaving this afternoon?"

"Yes."

"I'll let you know before you go."

"Thank you."

We were sipping a liqueur.

"Yes," the engineer said, wiping his forehead. "I always thought God didn't exist. But lately I have come to the conclusion that there must be something."

I guessed why he made this remark and answered: "I think so, too."

"Are you a Catholic?" he asked.

"Yes."

His wife came in and he began talking about the mine.

"Did you like it in the mine?"

"Oh yes; the most interesting part was the Joy. The people there are quite different, too."

Without knowing it, I had touched a soft spot. The Joy was his work.

"How do you mean?" he wanted to know.

"Well, the people there take pride in their work. They enjoy it more."

"You just have to know how to handle them. When we were about to open the Joy I called about thirty of the best workers together and said: 'We're going to start a new section with modern machines. They are expensive, and I'm going to entrust them to you. The exploitation of the new section will be your work. But on one condition: the wages will be good, but fixed. We can't pay by tonnage because no worker can keep up with those machines. It's up to you to decide if you want to come in or not.' They accepted, and now they consider it their own responsibility. The morale is excellent. After the first instructions I stayed away on purpose to show that I had confidence in them."

We sat down to lunch.

"Have you ever seen blueprints of the mine?"

"No."

"I'll show them to you after lunch in my study."

He did as he said, and explained the drawings.

"Do you know yet where you're going?"

"The director called St. Germain for me, but the director there was out and he has to call again."

"Just a moment."

He picked up the phone and called St. Germain. It was arranged: I could come.

"Where are you going this afternoon?"

"To Metz."

"Going out with a girl for a few days?"

"No, I have a good friend there."

"You can get a girl here, too, if you like."

"No, thank you."

"Come on, you want me to call?"

"Call?"

"Yes, what do you prefer, a blonde, a brunette or a redhead. Take your pick."

"I still have to settle some affairs here, and I won't have time."

"Come now, you have the whole afternoon."

He took the receiver off the hook and looked at me questioningly.

"No, thank you." I got up.

"Did you say good-bye to the director?"

"Yes, I did."

He shook hands with me. "The best of luck."

Marcel came with another friend. Lucien couldn't make it because of cramps in his leg. Hans came along, of course, and so did Klaus.

"Here's another technician!" I said, introducing Klaus to Marcel.

"You are?"

"Yes."

"Drop by some time, if you like!" Marcel invited him.

Max went by bus.

On the town square, where I was to take the bus to Metz, we met the foreman of the Joy. He joined us, too.

We drank one round, two rounds, three rounds.

It was time to leave. I got up to pay. But everything had been taken care of. Who had done that?

They shook hands with me, with all the firmness of men who load thirty tons of ore in six hours.

11

THE iron mine where I was going was in the region of the Meurthe and Moselle Rivers. But in Metz I heard that there was a fair coming and that I had better wait till it was over. That meant I had about a week off, which was very pleasant, for it was midsummer. I found a small, dilapidated hotel and took a fairly large, inexpensive room. It was furnished with a high, old-fashioned bed, a fancy, full-length mirror and a round table with one center leg. The wall between my room and my neighbor's was not very thick, so that I couldn't help overhearing what went on next door. My neighbor must have been living in the hotel for some time, and he was still there when I left. He took his meals alone and in silence at a table next to mine in the restaurant downstairs, and flirted with the waitress. He came home late at night and before long someone would join him. I heard giggling until I fell asleep, and sometimes I would be awakened by the sound of the door that wasn't closed carefully. *C'est la vie!* You don't have to read the book of Genesis to know that man and woman are made for one another and that it is not good for a man to be alone. You know it without thinking. Man and woman are attracted to each other beyond reason, almost as if the blood and all the tissues in their bodies reacted to one another.

The clergy is often reproached for acting as though spiritual care consisted only in the regulation of sexual life, which gives the impression that grave offenses are possible only in that sphere. In this way, heavy weather is made over things that would otherwise be regarded as quite harmless. The common belief is that everything which has to do with sex is condemned by people who lead repressed, celibate lives, and that in the studies of the moralists sins and temptations are invented which in reality are only part of the normal game of flirtation and the poetry of life. The latter objection is not wholly unfounded, and I have personally observed the feeling of liberation people experience when they are led to the true moral basis of the Ten Commandments. Nature must really keep those Commandments if it is not to destroy itself. When people believe in the will of God and the corresponding order of nature, and accept the principle that sexual satisfaction must be psychologically and biologically limited to the marriage union by virtue of the nature of reproduction and the purity of love, they will know in most circumstances what they may and what they may not do. The teaching of morality should concentrate on that doctrine, and not waste energy in spelling out very doubtful occasions of sin, since in this peripheral field whether something is an occasion of sin or not often depends on what one has been taught.

Meanwhile the sexual drive of man is so strong that in the course of spiritual care the clergy has no choice but to emphasize the restraint of it. But why codify the "game of seduction" and the "poetry of life" according to their sinfulness? A morally educated man can judge these things for himself. I believe that the occasions of sin decrease in proportion as a man advances in the consciousness of what constitutes the essence of both perfection and sin. And is not this what is meant by the "freedom of the children of God"?

The week I spent in Metz gave me the opportunity to say Mass regularly again. The awesome nature of it affected me most powerfully, since I had been so completely immersed in a material world. The altar and my feet now stood among the people for whose sake the sacrifice of Christ continues to be offered each day. This situation was not new to me but, although there was no essential difference, my awareness of it was stronger.

The priest of the church which I visited daily was the type of good shepherd who believed that at bottom all people were good. I didn't want to argue the point.

He often invited me to breakfast and would tell me of his many experiences. The alienation from the Church was not due to wrong spiritual care, he felt, but arose from the fact that society had changed. In the long run, eternal truth would triumph. This point I didn't want to argue, either. Confronted with venerable gray shepherds I always feel inferior. It was as if he wanted to make me feel that scientific research was not necessarily required for maintaining and propagating the Kingdom of God. And I didn't want to contradict him. What counts in the end is grace. Otherwise your towers are built on sand.

He was a gentle, friendly man who liked a good glass of wine and a good meal. He was wise in the notion that all human activity is relative, and he kindly let me go my own way without attempting to give counsel or advice.

All the same I stuck to my opinion that one should co-operate with grace, and that this collaboration may vary a great deal depending on time and place.

From Metz I went to visit the Gérard Nilences.

"I can't understand monastery life," Gérard said to me once.

"A priest like you at least deals with real life. If a monk's life should be like that, I could understand and appreciate it. And that people withdraw from the world in order to pray I can accept, too. I accept it on the authority of the Church, though I don't understand why the praying should have to be so incessant. But when people who live isolated from the world and are more or less strangers to it want to guide us, it can only end in failure. And there are too many like that. Don't you think most of the clergy are that way?"

"How would you want the clergy to live and work?"

"I don't know. But they don't feel or think like ordinary people. They are a class apart. Their behavior is so often strictly bureaucratic and authoritarian!"

"Do you think so?"

"Yes, and it's often so spiritual that people don't know what to make of their reasoning. There are exceptions, of course, such as the worker-priests. But on the whole the clergy belongs too little to the people. Take the seminary, for instance: the boys there are shut up like hothouse plants! They become unreal creatures, and that between the ages of twenty and thirty! What purpose does it serve? Let celibacy and the priesthood make the clergy into a class apart, into a different type of people with a dignity of their own, but does that mean they have to be alienated from society?"

"In a certain sense, yes. If you want to serve everybody and serve God, too, you don't belong to any class; you have to preach the truth as such. And that truth has to take its being from the nature of the people who are listening."

"That's just it. The application is left to the people themselves. I think priests should also preach the truth from the point of view of the people they are talking to. And they don't do that!"

"You exaggerate."

"All right, they don't do it enough, because they no longer live among or with the people, and therefore they don't think the way the people do."

"To give guidance is always more important than to identify with a certain group."

"Can't the two things be done at the same time?"

"Perhaps. But at any rate I don't agree with your statement that when the clergy teaches unassailable truths, it should apply them in detail to individual cases. At most they might use an actual case as an example. After all, every man has to learn to live according to his own sense of responsibility and the principles he accepts either intellectually or on faith. Everyone accepts a truth in his own personal way; his particular characteristics, his nature, his gifts give him a certain leeway and at the same time put upon him his own individual obligations. The priest should educate his people to Christian independence and not spell out every little detail of their lives. I even believe that this is one of the reasons why people have fallen away from the Church: the moralists of recent centuries have stifled them with this kind of trivia.

"To guide the people and be in close contact with them, fine! But to think exactly like the people, no, that is unrealistic. In the first place, what does 'to think like the people' mean? As far as I can see, there is only individual thinking, and emotionally no two people think alike."

"But don't you think there are some constant factors in emotional thinking which are found in entire groups?"

"Certainly, and they have to be taken into account. But guidance has to be mainly objective and must not become identified with a particular milieu."

The ladies had been listening to all this with sincere, impartial pity and with something like all-embracing concern. The hostess drew our attention to the fact that, unfortunately, the pudding hadn't turned out very well.

"How can you serve something like this?" someone asked, eating heartily of it.

I had heard Gérard's remarks before, with variations. People often object to the way the priestly function is exercised. When they don't come out with accusations of arrogance, greed, hypocrisy or sexual offenses, they still complain—as I had heard it put so clearly in Germany—that "the clergy and the people are like two railroad tracks that run parallel."

Isn't the priesthood a problem? If it is, the whole of Christianity is a problem. In that case one would have to say that Christ has made people problematical. Why?

In every heresy there is some truth that has been pulled out of its context. Insofar as heresy contains this truth, it is an indictment of the Catholic Church, which in a certain period did not give a certain truth or value its full weight. In spite of this reaction, the Church still retains the fullness of the truths and values revealed to her, for the simple reason that it is not the Church as the continuation of Christ's life in the world, but the Church as a community of people with weaknesses and limited conceptions dependent on time and place, that provokes these heresies. The faithful experience Christ in a limited way. This is an essential quality of the Church. Christ is always with the Church, and this constitutes its holiness; but there is also man in all his weakness, who is the reason the Church exists. As a number remains the same no matter how poorly and shakily it is written, so the holiness of the Church remains the same no matter how imperfectly it is manifested in the experience of its members.

Meanwhile it is a historical fact that the greater the attention given to details, the more the large body of truths that constitutes the Church threatens to recede into the background. One can become annoyed, for instance, with the formal carrying out of Church obligations which seems devoid of spiritual vitality—even to the extent that their low moral attitude toward life is in contradiction to the name of "Christian" that people bear. A reaction to this can lead to a break with all formalism. This is how Protestantism came into being. And thrown back on itself, it fell into one error after another. It remains true, however, that actual abuses in the Church contributed to the schism. Pope Adrian VI openly admitted this guilt with regard to the Reformers.

Protestantism can truly be considered a reaction to actual shortcomings in the Church as a human community. But other spiritual movements that have left the Church, either partially or completely, are also the result of such reactions. Is not liberalism in the broad sense of the word the result of too much restriction of human freedom?

Didn't the fact that the spirituality of the Church became too far removed from the world open the door to materialism? Pascal remarks in his *Pensées* that man's striving to be an angel results in his becoming a beast. This happens not only to the individual; the same striving in a society produces the same opposite result.

And isn't naturalism in the same way a reaction against a tendency in supernatural asceticism to violate nature to such an extent that its value as a creation of God is almost denied? The essence of the supernatural life itself is thus distorted, since the truth is that grace does not destroy nature, but pervades and elevates it.

Are nudism and the "back-to-nature" movement nothing but expressions of sick sensuality, or do they represent a revenge of nature on an ideal of holiness that denies the enjoyment of the human body?

Isn't Communism made possible by a too individualistic ideal of perfection, wherein love—which represents the equality of all people in Christ—is bought off with the easy performance of formal duties and with the practicing of an impersonal, systematized love for one's neighbor?

All these movements are at the same time anti-clerical, because the priest is considered pre-eminently the representative of the Catholic Church, and because he is held responsible for narrow-minded interpretations of the Christian way of life.

It is important to keep this in mind, lest we consider ourselves "persecuted people," to whom would apply the words of Christ that the disciple will fare no better than the Master.

A priest, like everyone else, is subject to his personal constitution and personal history, his country and the values prevailing in it, his education and upbringing, which are determined not only by the revealed doctrine of the Church but also by the times.

Now it is curious that though individual priests may fail and be narrow-minded, the priesthood as such, in its hierarchic tie with Rome, preaches Christianity in its fullness. Yet another curious thing is that although the times and the characteristics of peoples play a part in the way Christianity is experienced, the Church as the continuation of Christ preserves in its fullness the objective truth concerning human nature, Revelation, and the working of grace.

Where can one find the priesthood in its perfection and perfect Christianity? Nowhere . . . and everywhere. It is as with the soul. It cannot be found exclusively in one part of the body, but pervades the whole of it. This is also the mystery of the Church as the mystical body of Christ. When Priest X speaks, it is not the Church of God that is speaking; if Mr. Y realizes Christianity in his life, he is not the Church of God either. If the Pope in the fullness of his power defines a dogma, we hear the voice of God. But as a person he may share the weaknesses of humans bound by time and place; he has to confess his guilt to a priest, who then represents Christ to him. Christ is wherever the word of God is and wherever grace is. The word of God is the possession of the entire Church under the guiding principle of papal infallibility, and grace is wherever the sacraments and supernatural love are.

Whatever the truth contained in the strictures of Protestantism, materialism, liberalism, naturalism, the cult of nature, Communism and anti-clericalism, they do not touch the Church in its essence, but apply only to Catholicism in some of its concrete manifestations in certain times and places. And they do indeed contribute to the struggle for the freedom of the children of God by those elements in their doctrines which are not contrary to Christian truth or the natural law. The error of these systems and currents of thought consists in their being cut off from the whole body of Revealed Truth which, regardless of the errors of individuals, is kept intact in the Church of God.

The freedom of the children of God is the truth in grace and in nature, which often has to struggle free from the pressure of

a certain age, of a particular region, and from the pressure of
certain people, including priests insofar as they represent the
limitation of an individual. The truth will liberate us, but since
human limitations always are a factor, this liberation is a struggle
in every individual as well as in society as a whole; a struggle
that starts anew with each man and ends only in holiness and in
the possession of God. That is why Christ, as the Bringer of the
freedom of truth, did not come to earth to bring peace, but individual and collective struggle. And at the same time He did
bring peace, for peace comes through truth and love.

Christianity is not so much a problem as a tension. It is also
paradoxical, for it is in this world yet not of this world. This
aspect of it corresponds to human life, for this, too, is paradoxical:
bound to the world, man also transcends the world. The priesthood shares this tension to a high degree. In the first place because a priest represents a limited incarnation of Christianity. He
represents Christianity, but he *is* not the Revelation any more than
he *is* Christianity. The positive value of anti-clericalism lies in the
fact that it reminds us of this. Priesthood as such is nowhere
and everywhere, just as the soul is in the body and Christianity
is in the society of Christians. If one accepts this, anti-clericalism
is a necessary outcome of the dynamics of Christianity, namely
the struggle for freedom based on the full truth. I may have
well-founded objections to the interpretation by a certain priest
of certain truths and values. I may object to the way he realizes
Christianity in himself and wants it realized in others. The com-
parison of clergy and laity with two parallel railroad tracks represents a real problem which demands a solution. The reaction is
a genuine one, and it is healthy.

In the second place the priesthood evokes tensions because it
is inherent in its nature to be both leavening and salt. Leaven has
to be present in dough if it is to rise; but dough and leavening
resist each other until the yeasting process is finished. Salt is an
alien substance in the food that is to be salted. But if we only

put them side by side nothing happens; or the salt may lose its taste and the food may spoil.

A priest cannot identify with one single class. He is for everybody, and completely for everybody. He can be undividedly for one class only if the care of only one class is entrusted to him. But even then he must constantly take care not to be submerged in the emotional thinking of that group, and always be ready to serve others as well. Therefore there is something unreasonable in the demand that he must guide the people and at the same time be one of them.

Yet that isn't what people object to when they say that priests are often alienated from life. It's that the priesthood has become a force apart with its own life, which is not in harmony with its true nature. Priests live apart, they think apart, and have often become tangibly isolated. They—the salt—have become separated from the mass in many places. The mass is blamed for it, but I think that is a little one-sided. One looks everywhere for the causes of dechristianization, except in a certain devaluation of the priesthood. The cultivation of a particular clerical style, like that of a particular monastic style of life, is sometimes mistaken for the cultivation of holiness, whereas holiness bears no relation to formalism.

On the other hand the clergy cannot help being isolated to a certain extent because of its sacramental function in society. But this isolation is the opposite of an alienation of life. Therefore it might be better not to use the word "isolation" at all. It's better to speak of the spiritual distinction that is characteristic of the priesthood in relation to society; a distinction that may also be expressed in the clothing.

12

THE short break in my mineworker's existence had come to an end. I arrived in St. Germain on the last day of the fair. The workers were still off, but I was expected at the director's office. It was raining when I got off the bus rather early in the morning. I left my luggage in a barracks near the bus stop. A few hours later I found that I was to live in that very barracks.

St. Germain was very different from the workers' colony in Filondange. Friendly houses, all with front yards, well kept— in short, a park village. People later told me proudly that theirs was the second "neatest" village in France.

The mine itself, too, made a very different impression. The entrance was through a well-constructed arched gate. Next to it were the administration and accounting buildings. The worker didn't pass through the gate—only the heavy traffic did—but went by the administration building. They received their numbers in the office itself. This was only a small difference with Filondange, but psychologically significant. Next to the gate was a big parking place for bicycles. The roads leading to the main building and the shafts were lined with bushes like a park. The buildings themselves may not have been architectural masterpieces, but they were at least good-looking.

Since this mine came under the jurisdiction of Edouard Nilence, I had told him that I wanted to be treated like an ordinary worker in every respect. The engineer who received me in the director's absence had been thus informed. I was given working clothes and a locker like everyone else. After these first formalities I returned to the barracks where I had left my luggage. It was made of wood, but much more pleasant than my previous living quarters. There were several of these barracks, with only about twenty workers in each.

Since each barracks was administered separately, also for feeding, it was possible to lead a kind of "family" life under the good care of the woman in charge. The food was tasty and varied, and it was served to us. Every morning a packed lunch and a jar of coffee stood ready for us to take to the mine. There was running water, and the toilets were clean. The rooms, each shared by four people, were large. We had a closet and a chair each, and one table for the four of us.

When I came in I handed my papers to the woman in charge; she invited me to have a drink while she made the necessary arrangements.

I took a glass of wine and looked around me. A young fellow was leaning against the counter, an aperitif in his hand. He was watching me rather furtively. He was solidly built, but didn't have the swaggering manner of the "strong man" type. Apparently he had heard that I was to be his roommate. He seemed somewhat timid, yet interested in the newcomer. The woman called me to come along. She took me to my room, was very friendly and told me to ask her for whatever I needed. Then she left. The wooden walls of the room were painted a dark brown. There were four beds, and over one of them hung a picture of the Sacred Heart.

Soon the boy from the dining room came in. He mumbled a greeting and started looking for something in his closet. I went up to him and held out my hand, which he shook warmly.

"Frans," I said.

"Martin."

"Is this your bed?"

"Yes."

"Then we are roommates; this is mine!"

"Yes."

I continued unpacking.

"Are you coming to work here in the mine?" he asked.

"Yes, I am."

"St. Germain?"

"Yes. You too?"

"No, I work in Plasne."

"Where is that?"

"Near Boudrou."

"Oh," I said, no wiser.

"Underground?" he asked.

"Yes."

He was watching me as if he were glad I had come.

"Shall we have a drink to my arrival?" I asked when I had finished.

"Okay." He followed me back to the dining room.

"What would you like?" I asked him.

"Eh . . . ," He looked at the supply behind the counter, ". . . a Martini." Meanwhile he pretended it was all the same to him.

"Two Martinis!" The woman poured.

"Your health!"

"What's that?" I asked, pointing to a bottle with a branch in it.

"Fleur des Alpes . . . very good, don't you know it?"

"No."

"Two Fleur des Alpes," he ordered.

"Good," I said, emptying the glass. Some of the men had come in and were eating a hot lunch.

"Another round," he said. "No, let's have two Cointreaus."

They were put before us at once.

"Another round?" He didn't wait for my reply. "Two more!"

I wanted to pay, but he wouldn't hear of it.

"How much?" he asked the woman, and while she was adding up he ordered a third round of Cointreau.

After that we joined the other men for our meal. This was to be our regular group: Martin, an Italian, a Pole, a Yugoslav, and I.

They were ordinary workers. At another table three men were

seated: an older employee, an apprentice from the mining school named Paul, and a football player who, I was told, didn't lift a finger in the mine and felt it was beneath his dignity to talk to the workers when he was not in the mine. He had a well-paid job only because he was an excellent football player.

After lunch the player disappeared and a young boy by the name of Henri came to play cards with the other two. Martin joined them.

In the course of the afternoon Martin and Henri took me to the fair, but all we did was watch people driving small cars and bumping into each other. There wasn't much going on: the fair had lasted too long.

We went to bed early, for work in all mines started at 6 A.M., and the mine where Martin worked was half an hour's bicycle ride away. I hung up my coat, started undressing, and said to Martin: "I hope it doesn't rain tomorrow; this coat is too good to wear to work."

"I can lend you a coat." He got one out of his closet. "You can have shoes, too, if you want them."

"No, I'll put on my working shoes here."

"If you should need anything when I'm not here, just look in my closet and take anything you like."

"Thanks." (But during my stay in St. Germain I managed to get along with my own things.)

"Who sleeps there?" I asked, pointing to one of the two empty beds.

"The Italian." But he was usually late, left again early, and didn't show himself much.

"And over there?"

"My brother, but he comes only once a week. The other nights he sleeps over in Plasne."

In spite of the picture over his bed Martin got in without praying. To pray openly outside the church is not done among the workers, I found. And they hardly ever go to church.

The next morning we were awakened by a knock on the door. This was to happen every day. In the dining room a light breakfast was ready for me, as well as coffee and bread to take along. Dressed in my overalls and in heavy shoes I went to the mine. No one greeted me; no one knew me as yet. But the people who were around at that early hour looked perceptibly better than the workers in Filondange. Not only the houses, but the miners themselves looked more civilized.

I passed the administration building, got my number and walked through the little park to the building where the dressing and shower rooms were. Here, too, I was treated like an ordinary worker. I had a steel locker for my things like everybody else. But I didn't succeed in becoming a miner like the others any more than in Filondange. Not because the workers didn't consider me one of them, but because the foremen, here as in Filondange, were apparently set on letting me work as little as possible.

"Come along with me," said my boss. I had no choice but to follow him. The road and the steps to the shaft were covered. We waited our turn to go down into the dark pit. He asked me all sorts of questions: where I came from, why I came to work here, and so on. In spite of the fact that my answers didn't really tell him anything, he gave me only light work.

I was put with the *regie*, the crew who took care of the maintenance of the mine. Our mine was modernized to such an extent that there were hardly any places left where the ore had to be loaded by hand. I had to help put down rails, straighten them out with a wrench when they were bent, and put the links together. That wasn't particularly difficult. The only heavy work was the lifting and carrying. But there were enough of us so that we all could take a breather in turn. The idea seemed to be to do as little as possible and not to hurry: tomorrow was another day.

Before long the boss called me again. Did I speak English? he asked. Yes, I did. All right, would I please follow him? I did. A young miner who had picked up some English here and there was desperately trying with words and gestures to explain the workings of a particular machine to a visitor from England. It was too bad for the visitor that no one spoke English except some engineers who had no time for him. He was a student at an English technical college, but he had originally come from Africa and he was pitch-black. A friendly, polite boy who said little. He was going to stay for a few days and I was to be his interpreter. No easy task. In the first place the mine had its own slang that I couldn't translate into English, and in the second place my technical knowledge was so scant that I didn't understand many of the French explanations. But the visitor must have been cleverer than I, for every time I explained something to him that I didn't understand myself, he said enthusiastically: "Oh, I see." I didn't see anything. His visit, however, gave me the opportunity to go through the whole mine. Finally I returned to my rails.

The first thing that struck me about the workers in St. Germain was that they were generally more aware of themselves than the men in Filondange. This made them a little arrogant, too. They didn't have to be told anything. They all had their own views on life. Compared to them my previous comrades were really only children. They had a greater sense of unity, too. Here a man minded his own business and didn't mix too much with the others. Life in Filondange, in spite of the monotony and primitive conditions, had been a warmer thing. There had been a closeness that came from sharing the same fate, though the mass was more amorphous. Here I encountered "individuals" and a would-be culture: workers who had assumed the manners of the bourgeoisie, who insisted on their "rights" and whose feelings were easily hurt. In Filondange they had suppressed their grievances.

What was the cause of all this? It apparently had something to do with the civilized way the village was built and with the modernization of the mine. In the neighboring mines with their ill-kept workers' colonies, I found the same picture as in Filondange.

One of the previous directors of the mine in St. Germain had been a true philanthropist. He had done everything for his workers; he had had a beautiful village built, the like of which is seldom seen in France. And the present director had eliminated near-slave labor from the mine by mechanizing it. Yet the activity of the first director had come to a dead end in a would-be culture, and that of the second had succeeded only in encouraging pretensions among the workers. Something was lacking in the course of this development, that was obvious. It soon dawned on me that the spiritual growth of these people hadn't kept up with their material progress. Conditions were better in a material sense only. This is the easiest way, the way of least resistance.

These people, too, felt they were "only" workers. But they rebelled against it more. Sometimes they were hardly aware of the forms their rebellion took: for instance, they didn't notice how on pay-day they were exploited by merchants who took advantage of their naiveté and sold them rubbish at high prices. Fruit peddlers would sell them over-ripe, or even rotten, fruit they couldn't get rid of anywhere else, and for more money than their victims would have paid in town. But workers who have just been paid seem unconscious of the insult implied in this, and they spend their hard-earned money in a really foolish way. They almost feel sorry for the "poor guys" who would otherwise get stuck with their wares, and have come all the way from town to show them their merchandise.

In the mine itself they sensed more keenly that they were only workers. The older foremen were more authoritarian than in Filondange, and mechanization was seen only as a means of increasing production.

The job itself didn't give them a true "work spirit," and outside the mine there was no real culture.

Taken as a whole, they were still essentially simple people, no different from their colleagues in Filondange; but they had become accustomed to living in a reality colored by fireworks which they weren't mature enough to recognize as fireworks. They lived under the influence of their material surroundings.

The conversation among my fellow workers was as banal and immoral as can be imagined. Sex was discussed in the most vulgar

way. Sex was meant to be used, and whenever one felt the urge
for indulgence the most logical thing to do was to satisfy it. It
didn't matter how. Women and girls were created to fulfill this
need. There was much laughter and insinuation, as if to say:
Yes, yes, we know all about it; we're all made the same way, you
can't tell us anything new. If life didn't have that, it wouldn't be
worth living.

The sense of all being dirty together created a pleasant cama-
raderie. The presence of a boy of fifteen caused a lot of knowing
laughter. But they didn't have to worry about him, he knew all
about it, he was not a child any longer. All this moralizing of
priests and old women, that was nonsense. Besides, what purpose
did the God of the clergy serve? The God who had made them,
the workers, was apparently quite a different one. The Church
and the God of the Church were nothing but a money business.
"If your purse is full God is with you, if it's empty, the devil."

Meanwhile we carried, straightened, fixed and connected tracks,
or relaxed and talked about life. I listened. Their conversation
was dirty and pagan; but not to them. To them, this was reality,
though all they said of their experiences should be taken with a
grain of salt, for it was clear that each tried to outdo the other.

"The Church," said one of them, "is nothing but a clique.
Money and politics. We have to get back to the Bible, or this
world will go to hell."

I looked with so much surprise at the man who made this remark that the others hastened to protect me against him. I should
by no means get the idea that they agreed with him.

"There he goes again. He's worked on all of us, now he wants
to convert you."

"Convert me to what?"

They laughed knowingly.

But the fanatic went on. We had to serve God in spirit and in
truth, but the clergy had turned the Church into a gangsters'
hideout, and the Pope was the head bandit. He quoted texts left
and right. His co-workers let him go on for a while, listening

with bored faces. There was no stopping him. Finally the biggest
noisemaker said, somewhat irritated: "You sure have your own
Bible, haven't you?"

"There is only one Bible, but the clergy has falsified it."

"And you have the right one? Well, I don't know much about
the Bible. It leaves me cold. But I was baptized a Catholic and
that's good enough for me. It's not our business to figure out
which Bible is right and which is wrong."

The others laughed. Sure, that's how it was. The man sitting
next to me shrugged his shoulders indifferently.

"Do you have your own Bible, too?" I asked.

"Me? They can talk all they like as far as I'm concerned. I believe in nothing."

"That's not much."

He shrugged his shoulders again. We went on working, but the
fanatic gave me no rest. He rattled off one sermon after another.
Nobody felt like saying anything any more. They wished he'd go
to a mine somewhere far away on a desert island.

Crowded together like a herd of sheep, several hundred of us
were waiting at the shaft for our turn to be taken back into the
sunlight. Men pushed with their elbows to get closer to the shaft
cage. We were taken up twenty at a time, and on the surface
others were waiting to be taken down. Brown and dirty, we
noisily made our way down the iron staircase above ground in
our spiked shoes. In the shower room the first arrivals had already
stripped and were rubbing themselves clean with matter-of-fact
care—young fellows, their bodies tanned by the summer sun. But
this natural ease, taken for granted in their jobs, was not carried
over into their private lives. I had noticed that in the barracks my
roommates never undressed or changed clothes without first turning off the light. Yet in the shower rooms nudity was accepted
without question. It's a matter of custom without logic to it, and
no one will easily take the initiative that might change it. The
moral conscience of these boys is determined wholly by their
surroundings. For the same boys see nothing unusual in the cus-

tom of getting a girl every time they want to gratify the sex urge.
They simply do what everyone else does.

Once I had to cut up a piece of rock measuring several cubic
yards. The only tools I had were a sledge-hammer and a wedge.
I had been sweating over it for half an hour without success, and
my feeling of frustration was turning into rage, when a passing
miner saw my plight. I didn't know him, but he stopped and
watched me for a few moments. Then he came over and took the
hammer and wedge out of my hands: "This is the way you do it.
The grain of the rock goes this way." He placed the wedge, and
after a few strokes with the hammer a large piece of rock broke
off. "And here the grain goes this way." The grain was hardly
visible, but another piece of rock broke off. I wanted to take over,
for I had begun to understand the procedure. But he took
pleasure in it and cut the whole rock into pieces, so that there
was nothing left for me to do.
"Here you are."
"Thanks."
We smiled and he left.

In contrast to Filondange, most foremen in St. Germain were
young men between twenty-five and thirty. They were jovial and
friendly. The workers liked them better than the older ones. Their
orders were carried out without question, though they may not
always have had the necessary experience. One day one of them
took me with him. His name was Louis. His section was completely mechanized, and the work went smoothly. The pneumatic
drilling was not done by hand but automatically from iron scaf-
folding. All the workers had to do was to place the drills correctly
and control the process.
At that rate thirty-six holes several yards deep were drilled in
no time; then the drilling scaffolds were rolled away, the holes
filled with dynamite and connected by cables. Louis came with
an accumulator which was kept a few corridors away, the con-

nection was made, the alarm sounded, and with a thundering
noise as if heaven and earth were coming down, the wall burst
apart in a thirty-six-fold explosion. American scrapers and loading cars quickly cleaned up the piles of ore, and the drilling installations were put ready in front of another wall. We couldn't
see a yard ahead because of the dust and smoke. But there was
no question of waiting until ventilation had cleared the air. Groping and shuffling, I found my way back to where the boys were
working. They were nervous, and their headlamps seemed almost
extinguished in the thick dust. Little was said. That was part of
the job: you had to show you were a man. But sometimes it would
become too much.

One of the boys, his eyes moist with suppressed rage—and not
just from the smoke—would suddenly snap at me: "They should
put 'em in jail, the murderers!" He tinkered with his drilling machine. Hardly able to control himself, he got up again, stood in
front of me and shouted: "You call that modernization?" He
turned, as if to show me the situation. "And we can drop dead
for all they care! Production, money! In a few years we're done
for, we're finished, but I'm only twenty-eight!"

He was almost crying. Suddenly he was embarrassed, as if he
had behaved like a little boy, as if someone had caught him at a
weak moment. For a little while no one knew what to do or say.
Then it was over, as though nothing had happened. I went back
to work.

"The ventilation here isn't what you'd call excellent," I said to
Louis.

"Yet it works well enough," he replied. "Within fifteen minutes
or half an hour at most, everything is clear again."

"Yes, but then another section is full of dust."

"They make the ventilation as effective as possible. They're
improving it again now. All in all, it isn't so bad."

The miners themselves showed the same attitude. They were
even proud of the great things that had been accomplished.
Theirs was one of the most modern iron mines. Miners had to

take the disadvantages with the advantages. Meanwhile not one of them believed that modernization was done for the sake of the workers.

13

GRADUALLY I got to know the mine. I went with one foreman one day and with another the next. The layout and working methods varied a great deal in the different sections. I made the acquaintance of Gilles, a foreman aged twenty-six. He didn't like to have me work—since all I wanted was to know the mine, there was no reason why I should work. He doubted whether I was in full possession of my reason when I asked him to put me with the maintenance crew, as there wasn't much for me to do in the mechanized areas. But he agreed. It was my own business. However, it didn't last long.

He met me as I was dragging a very heavy piece of machinery through the corridor with another worker. It was hanging over a rod, and we had put the rod on our shoulders. After a few hundred yards I couldn't stand the pain and had to stop to change shoulders. My co-worker got a scolding. What was the matter with him, starting a newcomer on such work! The boy said nothing and went away. I felt sorry for him.

"You idiot," laughed Gilles, "come along with me."

His section was fairly large, and provided with some of the latest gadgets. He had, for instance, an electronic apparatus to measure the pressure on the rock walls. Iron clamps had been

attached in various spots in the corridors. When they were connected to the apparatus by wires, the pressure on the wall was
translated into sound. So if *do* were the normal tone, *fa* would
indicate something very dangerous.

He invited me to accompany him on a tour of inspection and
asked me many questions as to why I was in the mine.

"I'm studying the non-technical side of the work."

"What is that?"

"The human side."

"What do you mean by that?"

"The influence of this kind of work on people; how they can
develop in their work; how the work interferes with real human
needs; in short, the human problems of the worker's world."

"And why are you doing that?"

"Because I'm interested in the fate of the workers."

"But how much do you earn that way?"

"No more than what I earn by my own work."

"Can you live on that?"

"If the workers can live on it, I can, too. I live exactly as
they do."

"Where do you eat?"

"In the barracks."

"And where do you sleep?"

"Also in the barracks."

"My God, some undertaking. Do you like it?"

"That's not important. If I want to know what a worker's life
is like, I have to live it."

"And can you get a good job later with all that information?"

"That's not important either."

"Not important?"

"No. The main thing is to look after the workers' interests."

"It's terrific, but you'll get married some day and then you'll
need some kind of job. Or do you have money of your own?"

"Not much more than what I earn."

"It's beyond me. I could never have imagined anyone doing

this kind of thing, except a missionary or a priest maybe. You're pretty high-minded."

"I see life as it is, and as it can be, for myself and others. You may be a simple miner or something else, doesn't matter what. We all depend on each other, and it's hard to say who is more important. But I like life my way as everyone likes it his way, and together we form society, and in society we have to appreciate each other. Since I've worked and lived with the workers, I've come to admire them and really love them."

We were walking through the dark corridors, he with a head-light, I with a small carbide lamp.

"May I ask you something?" he said.

"Why not?"

"Come and have dinner with me tonight."

"On one condition."

"What?"

"Don't mention this conversation to anyone."

"I understand."

In Gilles' section there was a Spanish worker, a standard type. I would have known him among a thousand Frenchmen. A kind, cordial fellow with a warm voice. When I talked with him Spain came alive again for me.

"How did you get here?" I asked him.

"Civil war. Refugee."

"You never went back to visit?"

"No. It's impossible."

"Impossible? Why? If you haven't committed any crimes, it's quite possible."

"Is it?" That was news to him. "I was an ordinary soldier, that's all," he said.

"Then you can get back to Spain, at any rate to visit your family."

"I'd like to go, but they all say you can't get past the border."

"That's propaganda. I know several people who went back."

"But even my family writes I shouldn't come."

"It's difficult to find work in Spain. There's a lot of misery."

"If I weren't married, I'd like to go anyway."

"Don't you like it here?"

He shrugged his shoulders.

"Have you worked in the mine ever since the civil war?"

"Yes. We were put in a camp, and after a while they promised us our freedom if we'd go and work in the mines. I accepted."

How he liked to talk about Spain! More and more I believe that the difference between children and grown-ups isn't so great, and more and more I'm fascinated by the thought that we are all basically the same, whether we study theology or work in a mine.

Once, when I was working with the maintenance crew, an older foreman passed by. He was one of the dictator type. He could only snarl his orders, and was always showing off his superiority. He looked at me as a field marshal would look at a recruit. During the conversation that followed I could hardly keep from smiling.

"What are you doing here?" he growled.

"You can see what I'm doing." I was turning screws.

"How long have you been here?"

"Two weeks."

"Who put you here?"

"The chief foreman."

"What's the matter with him?"

"I don't know."

"Where are you from?"

"From Holland."

"From Holland?"

"Yes."

All of a sudden he was plainly interested. "Why don't you work in my section?" he wanted to know.

"That's not up to me."

"Tomorrow you come to me!"

The next day I had to go through his section with him. It was the oldest section of the mine, cold and damp. He found fault with everyone's work, but the boys laughed behind his back.

"Have you ever worked in an iron mine before?" he asked me.

"Yes, in Filondange."

"Who was the manager there?"

I mentioned his name.

"How was he?"

"Oh, all right, I believe. I didn't have much to do with him."

"Impossible. A man without experience. He got in through connections. A war buddy of the engineer. I should have got that job."

"Really?"

"Sure. But I told 'em good-bye. I don't need them."

"Is it better here?"

He didn't reply, but suddenly he became very friendly, as if we were old pals. I was surprised at the switch.

"You're from Holland, are you?"

"Yes."

"I'm not French either."

"No?"

"No, I'm from Luxembourg. Holland, yes . . . ."

"Have you ever been in Holland?"

"No, but it's well known, windmills and tulips . . . ."

"I come from the part where they grow the tulips."

"Do you? I've got some tulips in my garden, but not many."

"Have you got a big garden?"

"Yes, and a beautiful house, too. Drop in and have a look some day. I make my own mirabelle, the real stuff. Have you ever tasted it?"

"Yes, it's a plum brandy, a specialty of Metz, isn't it?"

"Yes, but you've never had the real thing. They don't make it any more. I'll let you taste some real mirabelle. Where do you live?"

"In the barracks."

"In the barracks? That's right near me. I'm one street further, on the other side of the railway. Are you in Bruscolini's barracks?"

"Yes."

"Is it okay there?"

"Oh yes, fine."

I stayed only one day in his section. But to my surprise he came to the barracks to have a drink the following Sunday. He treated me to drinks in grand style, much to the surprise of my friend Martin, who got his share of this generosity since we were together.

"When are coming to visit me?" the foreman inquired.

"Whenever it's convenient to you."

"Any afternoon is all right."

"Let's make it tomorrow afternoon," I suggested. He left, satisfied.

The housekeeper couldn't get over it. "I've never seen anything like it. Most newcomers don't say a word the first few weeks, and he behaves as if he's been here for months."

"That's how it should be," said Martin.

The next afternoon I went to see the foreman. He showed me the garden.

"Shall I send you some bulbs when I'm back in Holland?"

"Oh, I'd love that." He was happy as a child.

We drank mirabelle and he made me a present of a whole bottle. We talked till we came to the subject that interested me most.

"Is Luxembourg all Catholic?"

"Just like here."

"How do you mean?"

"People don't care much for the Church."

"You mean the workers?"

"Yes."

"You mean they don't believe any more?"

"Well, maybe they do, but that church business, that's nothing for us."

"Why do you stay Catholic then?"

"We don't do much about the Church and the clergy, but we know how far we can go. When it comes to belonging to the Church, we don't argue. It goes without saying that we have our children baptized and get a Catholic burial."

I saw that he didn't like the subject, so we changed the conversation.

Martin was the incarnation of goodness. He liked nothing better than to pay for others, and did it inconspicuously. He had no dependents. His parents had died and he had a good salary. His strength had become legendary from the time he had lifted some dump-carts back on the tracks after a derailment, when all efforts with levers had failed. Yet he didn't give the impression of a Hercules. Everyone liked him. Practically nobody took advantage of him, and he was warned against those who did. Most workers have too much sense of pride to be parasites.

Sometimes we were both on the morning shift, and then we would spend the afternoon together. But when he was on the afternoon shift and I finished at two o'clock, I had a hard time getting to bed at night, for he wouldn't let me go. He would come home about 10 P.M., and first, of course, we had to have a drink. After that we had to do something else.

"Don't go to bed yet, if you wait a minute I'll come with you," he would say. But the minute would turn into an hour, for he could sleep late the next morning. Usually we would sit with the card players, among whom was Paul, the apprentice, and another dignified but jovial employee. The latter was a quiet, amiable man of about forty-five, conscious of his superior wisdom. One evening, between games, he asked me: "Do you have a piece of paper?" I took out my notebook. "I'll write something beautiful in it," he said. And he wrote:

> "J'ai été maintenant
> ce que je suis à présent;
> cendres et poussières.
> J'ai cherché à me repaître
> des délices de ce monde
> et me voilà
> la pâture des vers."

He gave me back my notebook. I read it while he went on playing. "It's from an old French writer," he informed me.

Such literature was not exactly our daily fare. Yet it was written with an earnest and heartfelt melancholy. Meanwhile the brother of our housekeeper was dancing with his two-year-old daughter who shouted gaily:

> "Sur le pont
> d'Avignon
> l'on y danse, l'on y danse. . . . "

Another good friend of ours was Berto. He was an Italian by descent but born in France and a French citizen. He didn't live in the barracks with us, but he was Martin's best friend, and that was a good recommendation.

One beautiful afternoon he dropped in before dinner.

"You want to come along?" he asked us.

"Where to?"

"It doesn't matter. It's too beautiful to stay in."

"Shall we go for a bicycle ride?" suggested Martin.

"Are you crazy? It's much too hot."

"Then what shall we do?"

"Let's go fishing."

"Fishing?" I said. "Sit the whole afternoon on the river bank and catch nothing? I can't take that."

He was in a good mood; he rolled up his sleeves and asked: "You feel like boxing?"

"It's much too hot," I protested.

"Much too hot, my foot!" He grabbed me and I had to play the game. We fought, and finally, almost choking, I was thrown onto the bed. Martin cheered.

"Help!"

"What's the matter?"

"I'm choking!"

"No, you're not!"

I rolled off the bed, still fighting. My rosary fell out of my pocket. He let go of me.

"You could break a man in two," I said, picking up my rosary. He didn't seem to notice it.

"Don't ever get into a real fight with me," he laughed, "you might get messed up."

We were both panting. He sat down.

"Once I beat up a guy. Man, that wasn't funny."

"Is he still alive?"

"My God, man, was I mad. You know I have an Italian name. Well, when I had to go into the service, one of my buddies called me 'Macaroni.' If they hadn't held me, I think I would have murdered him. He was a lousy little squirt. He just wanted to show off. I told him he'd better make himself scarce for a while. But the fool came back and said it again. Then I let him have it. I practically beat him to a pulp. He didn't move when I was finished with him. Hah—the funny thing is that afterward we became friends."

"So we're going fishing, are we?" I inquired.

"Sure, why not?"

"But what about rods?"

"Who needs rods? We'll use forks."

"Fish with a fork? How do you do that?"

"You'll see."

We went out. Near St. Germain ran a little brook. You could jump over it without a pole and wade across it.

"You stay on the bank for a while and catch the fish we throw you," Berto told me. He rolled his trousers above his knees and stepped into the brook. Martin did the same thing.

"Here's where they are, you see, under the stones."

They threw me a fish, and another one, and another one. It went smoothly.

"We'll fry 'em later. They're very good."

I stepped into the water, too. The bottom was uneven and rather slippery. After a while all three of us were pretty wet.

"Don't you want to try?" Martin asked.

"Let's go and get our bathing trunks," I suggested.

"No, no," Berto replied decidedly, "we can't do that."

"Why not?"

"It's not done here. It's not decent."

I was surprised. We were in the middle of cornfields! The logic of the "decency" rules of the workers' world was still beyond me. Every day we saw each other in the shower; at home undressing in the presence of others was carefully avoided; in the swimming pool the men shared one dressing room; yet in the brook you couldn't even show yourself in bathing trunks. Anyway, we enjoyed ourselves that afternoon and returned home with a rich catch.

"Oh," exclaimed the housekeeper in consternation, "what have you been doing? You're not supposed to fish around here, you know that!"

"Come on," Berto said, "as long as the police don't catch you."

When the fish were fried, things became lively.

"Wine!" Martin called.

"*Boire un petit coup, c'est agréable,*" Berto started singing, "*To drink a little glass is very pleasant.*" The others joined in:

> "Boire un petit coup, c'est doux
> Mais il ne faut pas rouler dessous la table,
> Boire un petit coup, c'est agréable,
> Boire un petit coup, c'est doux."

The fish were served, almost a hundred of them. "We'll never manage all that," I said with some awe.

"Eat!" commanded Berto.

We ate and we drank and we sang.

> "J'aime le jambon et la saucisse,
> J'aime le jambon, c'est bon.
> Mais j'aime encore mieux le lait de ma nourrice,
> J'aime le jambon et la saucisse,
> J'aime le jambon, c'est bon."

Martin got into high spirits and sang his heart out:

> "Allons dans les bois, ma Mignonnette,
> Allons dans les bois du roi,
> Nous y cueillerons la fraiche violette,
> Allons dans les bois, ma Mignonnette,
> Allons dans les bois du roi."

And to Berto he sang:

> "Non, Lucien, tu n'auras pas ma rose,
> Non, Lucien, tu n'auras rien,
> Monsieur le curé a défendu la chose,
> Non, Lucien, tu n'auras pas ma rose,
> Non, Lucien, tu n'auras rien."

Berto and I made a date to go cycling the next day. Martin had to go to Plasne and couldn't come along.

We cycled for a few hours until we came to the woods. Then we took a rest in a meadow in between two hills.

"Look over there—terrific!" Some young men were doing exercises. They did them very well. Berto was excited and drew my attention to the feats of the limber boys.

The conversation became personal. He unburdened his heart about the hardships of a worker's life.

"Yet St. Germain is very well laid out," I remarked.

"Yes, but there's nothing going on."

"But you have a recreation center."

"Yes, but it's not used much, only for movies on Sunday."

"What about sports?"

"I love to play football."

"What about swimming? There can't be many villages that have their own swimming pools, like St. Germain."

"The pool isn't used much. The water is usually too cold. It comes from under the mine."

"Then what do you do all day?"

"The same as you. Work, sleep, eat, drink with the others, play football. And then . . . yes, I'm only an ordinary worker, but I like to read."

"Novels?"

"What I like best is those popular scientific articles. I like to know what the world is like and how different things are explained. And also, I love sports."

"Do you have enough money for all that?"

"Oh yes, I earn enough and I don't have to send much home. By the way, how much do you get?"

"I haven't been paid yet. I guess they'll give it to me when I leave. I'm only here for a little over a month, to get to know the mine, as I told you."

"But how can you get along?"

"I just have to be careful."

"Why didn't you say so before? I can easily spare some money."

"I think I can manage."

"Are we friends or aren't we? I don't want you to be short. We've got to help each other. I'll do it gladly."

"And suppose I can't give it back?"

"So what? My God, don't worry about that. Let's see, what if I gave you thirty thousand francs?"

"Are you crazy? If I have to pay that back before I leave, I'll be worse off than I am now."

"Don't pay it back then."

"Are you such a capitalist?"

"No, but why shouldn't I give it to you if you need it. I can get along. I earn good money. You don't even know how much you're going to get. Besides, what are you going to live on when you leave, before you've found other work?"

"That's just why I'm careful now. Anyway, I don't have to live in luxury. As long as I can manage."

"No, Frans, that's no good. Do me a favor and take that money. It's well spent on you. If you can pay it back, okay, if you can't, okay too."

"No, Berto, no!"

"Why not?"

"No."

We were lying beside each other in the grass. I was overwhelmed by so much goodwill.

"You're a funny guy. I haven't insulted you, have I?" he asked.

"No."

"Well then, what's all the fuss about?"

"The average worker doesn't have a friend like you," I replied. "He has to manage all by himself."

"But an average worker doesn't have the kind of life you have."

"Some of them are worse off than I."

"Frans. . . ."

"Yes."

"There aren't many guys like you." He thoughtfully pulled out one blade of grass after another. "I could never have thought that someone like you would be friends with me. I'm only a simple guy, you know." I looked at him. ". . . . I'm only a worker."

"And what about me?"

"I don't know, I'm confused . . . ."

For a while neither of us spoke.

"Is there a priest in St. Germain?" I asked suddenly.

"How did you get on that subject? Yes, of course there is."

"I've never seen him."

"Oh, he's a good man."

"What's the situation here? Do people still care about religion?"

"What's the matter with you? Of course they care."

"You too?"

"Me? I've nothing against the Church. Why should I?"

"I'm just asking."

"Hah, I used to be an altar boy. I got along fine with the priest."

"And now?"

"Now? What would I want with a priest? I'm not ready to get married yet."

"No."

"Well then, what do you want? I don't go to church, but that doesn't mean I'm not a Catholic. Do you go to church?"

"Yes."

"Here too?"

"I haven't been here on a Sunday yet."

"You can't very well go to Mass here."

"Why not?"

"Nobody goes. Only children. When I was little I used to go, but not afterward. Nobody does. Only the director and a few engineers."

"And what if everyone went?"

"Then I'd go, too."

"You don't dare to go by yourself?"

"Would you want to be a show-off?"

"No, but there are people who say that the workers no longer believe."

"Who says that?"

"People."

"That's not true. I've never given it much thought, but I don't think there are many who don't believe."

"I'm not sure."

"But is that a reason to go to Mass? I'm happy, and I'm grateful to God for that. And when I'm very happy I pray: 'Dear God, make all people as happy as I am.' I do that very often."

"And if you wanted to go to Mass, you wouldn't dare because of the others?"

"What do you think I am? I'm only an ordinary guy."

"I'm just asking. You don't mind, do you?"

"Oh no, go ahead." We cycled back and had a drink together.

That night, when we were already in bed, the Yugoslav came in dead drunk and started chattering. Martin didn't pay much attention to him. Finally he left. The next day he couldn't remember a thing.

The Pole was a ladies' man. When he told his stories he smacked his lips from pure sensuality. One morning he and I left together for the mine. A young girl walked in front of us.

"See those legs?" He smacked his lips with delight.

"Yes."

"Boy, do I love to look at women's legs!"

"Even early in the morning?"

"Oh yes, always."

14

IN THE swimming pool I met the workers' athletic coach. I started talking to him about sports in St. Germain. He was somewhat arrogant, but otherwise very frank. Yes, St. Germain was an ideal village, he said. "Thanks to Director X. When he was here, things were fine. Everybody got what he was entitled to. He did everything for his men. At the beginning of the war we got another one."

I gathered that this was the present director-general, who had helped me get my job.

"He wanted to know whether his people were good Catholics before he would take 'em on," the coach continued. "But what does religion have to do with work? The director we have now is interested only in mechanization. And if you know somebody high-up, it helps. If you're a good football player you can easily get a job. I like sports myself, but that's not fair."

"The workers can't complain about their wages, as far as I can tell."

"No, unless they work in maintenance or above ground. The others get enough. But everybody can get enough as long as he breeds children. You get half again as much salary if you have a child. Crazy."

"Why?"

"Because people who don't want children have to pay that much in taxes. Let everyone live the way he likes is my motto."

"You don't have any children yourself?"

"Yes, I have a boy."

"Where do you live?"

"Rue de la Marne."

"Oh, there."

"Have you ever been there?"

"I've passed through," I said, "but I don't know what the houses look like inside."

"Come and have a look, if you like. Some people spend their money on liquor and tobacco. I don't drink and I don't smoke, but I've arranged my house the way I want it."

"I'd very much like to see it."

I could see that he was pleased. "When can you come? Tell me when it's convenient," he urged.

"Tomorrow night? Or are you on the afternoon shift?"

"No, tomorrow night is fine. But I'm on the same shift as you!"

"Are you?" I asked in surprise. "I've never seen you."

"Yes, you have. You were in our *chantier* once with Gilles. We have that new scraper, the one you can work from a distance."

"Is that where you work?"

"Yes. Do you understand how the scraper works?"

"Not very well. We were there only for a few minutes."

"Come again some day, I'll explain it to you."

"Gladly."

While we were lying peacefully in the sun, the church bell began to ring.

"What's that for?" I asked.

"How should I know? I'm not interested in that sort of thing."

"Aren't you a Catholic?"

"Me?" He shrugged his shoulders. "There are still people who want the what-you-may-call-it . . ."—he pointed in the direction of the church—"to keep going. What purpose it serves, I don't know. The director and the others go only for their own salvation. My wife goes to church, too, once in a while. I guess because she's afraid."

"Afraid of what?"

Again he shrugged his shoulders. "I'm not a believer myself."

"How do you mean?"

"Well, I do believe in God, of course, but not in that other business."

"Oh."

"Why should I? They're against us, anyway."

"You mean the Church here is against the workers?"

With another shrug he explained: "Once they were behind us when we went on strike. Then they were all right, and for a short while we thought the Church was really on our side. But it didn't last long. And now it's again like it always was. No . . ." Thoughtfully he gazed into the sky.

The next evening I went to see him. Proudly he showed me his home, which really looked beautiful. He was obviously pleased that I liked it.

"You have an expensive radio."

"That's because I economize, my friend!"

We were served wine and cakes.

"What," I asked in surprise, "what do you mean, economize? I thought you didn't drink."

"When you come I do!" He did his best to treat me royally. I like this naive joy, which comes out in everyone at times.

One afternoon, when I returned from the mine, Martin was home.

"What's the matter, is there a strike?"

"Yes!"

"Why?"

"The ventilation and the pumps don't work. We were wading in water and the smoke was suffocating us. It was impossible to go on working. The boss wouldn't let us go, but the son of the director works in our section and he said we were right. The inspector came and said the same thing. So I have a few days vacation. That mine of ours is a bitch, though. You're lucky you work in St. Germain."

"Why did you leave here?"

"Leave? You think you can just leave a mine like that? No, if you did, you'd have a tough time finding other work. No other mine would take you on."

"Then how did you get to Plasne?"

"Because St. Germain had to lay men off. That's a different thing. I found another job in no time. A dirty trick it was, too. They said it was because of mechanization. Everybody hired within the last few years was put out in the street, without discrimination. But a few weeks later they were hiring new personnel. Figure that one out, if you can. Of course what they wanted was to get rid of a few guys that were no good, and the others had to pay for it. Then they wanted me back again. But I'm not that crazy! They'd better not get the idea they can do whatever they like with us."

I knew that the men in St. Germain would like to have Martin back, including the foreman. He was a first-rate worker and a good friend. I had heard more than once that he'd made a mistake in staying on at Plasne; that he would be welcomed back in St. Germain with open arms. But he had his pride! He would always grow a little melancholy when he talked about such things, saying, "It was unjust!" He couldn't take that.

We stood drinking at the counter. It was all part of life, he said. And would I please not think of paying. Maybe one round at most, just to save my honor. For I must understand, he didn't want to offend me. We were getting along like brothers, weren't we? So would I please dispense with formalities. Why, when he was on the afternoon shift he took my dirty laundry on Monday morning!

"Give me my bill, will you?" he asked the housekeeper. "It's time I settled with you."

The housekeeper, who trusted him one hundred percent, began to add in her head. The bill was for a whole week, and that was no small matter.

"Four plus four, plus seven, plus another four, plus three, twenty-four glasses of wine . . . fifteen Cointreaux . . . twelve Martinis . . . let's see, what else?"

"Fleurs des Alpes," Martin added. "How many?"

"I don't know, one, three, seven . . ."

"Don't you cheat me," the housekeeper warned, "or you'll end up in hell."

He was still on edge because of the strike, and he snapped: "Don't bother me with your hell! Tell me how much I owe! I don't have to keep track of it, do I? And when did I ever cheat you?"

"Oh, I didn't mean it that way," the good woman said, quite upset.

"Then tell me how much it is."

He paid casually, with a rather shamefaced grin. "That's my life for you," he might have been saying, but we strolled away without comment.

"Would you like to go with those two this morning?" the chief foreman asked when I arrived in the mine section where the work was assigned and the trains started.

"Yes, let him come with us," one of the boys who heard him said. "Come on, let's get going."

"It'll be a day to remember," he added smiling as our train thundered through the dark corridors.

"Why? What's up?"

"You'll see."

At an intersection about ten of us got out. Another train, with some dump carts attached, stood waiting. We threw in our things and got in ourselves, then rode quite a distance through a fairly deserted section. There was no illumination; we could see each other only by the light of our own lamps.

Finally the train stopped. "Here we are," my friend said. The three of us jumped down and took our tools. The others went on.

We turned into a side corridor, walking in single file. The uneven rock walls flickered dark brown in the light of our lamps. On one side of us water babbled in a ditch, on the other ran some railway tracks. We walked for almost fifteen minutes though a labyrinth of corridors before arriving at our destination.

Guy, the leader, put down his lamp. Raymond, his chief assistant, did the same. I saw that we were standing in a large, high, eerie vault. Against one of the walls lay a pile of ore several yards high.

Guy attached the hose of his pneumatic drill to the compressed air supply; Raymond inspected the ceiling.

"It's dangerous here," he said.

"Why?"

"The ceiling is loose, and we can't be sure of it."

"Come on, nothing will happen," Guy said.

"It's the most dangerous *chantier* in the mine," his friend protested, "and you're the greatest daredevil of us all."

"The more you complain, the more dangerous it gets," Guy laughed. He climbed on top of the ore pile and put his drill into the rock. He set the drill under the full weight of his body, watching the ceiling out of the corner of his eye.

We didn't have to load; scrapers would do that later. All we had to do was to break up the big chunks with a pick-axe or a sledge-hammer.

Soon we were able to detonate our first explosion. After the second explosion we went to have our lunch a few corridors away. The three of us sat on a tool kit. A short distance from us another explosion was set off, and in the light of our lamps we soon saw a thick cloud of smoke coming toward us. We fled.

"He's afraid," Guy said matter-of-factly, taking a bite of bread.

"Yes," Raymond admitted, "I'm scared to death of silicosis."

"We've been working together for years," Guy went on. "I know him."

"I know *him*, too," said Raymond. "Whenever there are dirty jobs to be done, he's the man for it. And I have to go with him."

"That's not true. Sometimes *I* have to go with *you*. A good thing, too."

"Why?" I asked.

"Once we had to work in a place just like this. While he was drilling, I saw that the roof was loosening over his head. I ran to him, grabbed him and pulled him away at the very moment the whole business caved in. It sure was in the nick of time. He hadn't noticed a thing."

"No," Raymond said with his mouth full.

"A good thing the roof did come down, otherwise he'd have bawled me out for grabbing him for nothing."

"Yes," Raymond admitted with a smile.

"Listen to him, he even says so! He's been living on borrowed time now for a year and a half. He should really give me half his wages. But do you think he ever would?" He grabbed his friend by the shoulder and they started cavorting about. The smoke passed by our new hideout, but it was thinner now and we could stay where we were.

"One thing is sure," Guy said, "my children won't go into the mine."

"How many children do you have?" I asked.

"Two. I hope to be able to give them enough so they can make their way through life. I'm thirty-five now, and I'll hold up for a few more years."

"Have you always worked here in the mine?"

"Oh no, I was in Paris first. I've been here for nine years. Not that it's so wonderful here, but at least you earn some money."

Guy was witty and athletic. The fifteen-minute lunch break passed much too quickly. We went back to work, and in spite of the apparent danger nothing went wrong. Toward the end of

the shift some miners came from the other *chantiers* to go with
us to the train. Raymond put our tools in the kit and I stood
talking at the entrance of the *chantier* with the boys who had
just arrived. We watched as Guy rolled up the hose of his drill
and picked up some more tools. Suddenly we all stood as if
nailed to the ground. For a fraction of a second there was dead
silence, then something moved in the roof. There were cries,
there was a sound of creaking, and an enormous piece of the
roof fell with a thundering impact on the exact spot where Guy
had stood. But he had noticed the danger at the same time we
had — everything had happened in a split second — and he
had jumped aside against the wall. His lamp had gone out. He
lit it again, lifted it to investigate the hole in the roof and, un-
ruffled, went back to gathering his tools.

"It always happens to you!" one of the men exclaimed, shaking
his head.

"You're lucky you're alive, man," said another.

"Yes, yes," Guy replied simply. He smiled a little. "I'm not
afraid to die." He lifted the hose onto his shoulders. "Not that
I'm anxious to die. I have a wife and children. But if my time
has come and the good Lord wants it . . . then I can only say:
Thy Will be done. He'll look after my wife and kids."

Was it a monologue or was he talking to us? No one said anything, as if his explanation were the most logical thing in the
world. He came out of the brown darkness of the cave and joined
us, and we started back.

I was walking next to him. For the first few minutes not a
word was said. Then he suddenly asked me: "Do you believe
in God?" I was startled by this unexpected question.

"Yes, I do."

Another silence. The water in the ditch beside us made its
peculiar ripping sound. We strode on in the semi-darkness, following the lights of our friends ahead of us.

"Do you believe very, very much?"

He looked at me sidewise. A beautiful, dirty-brown, smiling

face with a touch of mystery, seen in profile — was it an effect
of the lighting or was it the question that produced this look?
I felt something like a pain inside me when I answered: "I hope
my belief is strong enough."

"I believe very, very much," he said seriously.

"It's faith that gives life meaning," I said.

Again he looked at me for a moment and mumbled to himself:
"Very true, it's faith that gives life meaning."

Not another word passed between us. The trains and the shaft
were, as usual, very crowded.

15

BERTO invited us to have dinner at his home on Saturday night.
His parents were away on vacation, so he was his own boss. We'd
spend a nice evening among friends, he said. He would ask Paul
too, and Pierre, his neighbor. There would be five of us. Fine,
said Martin.

Berto came on his bicycle to fetch me. Why weren't we there
yet? he wanted to know. Paul had already arrived.

"Martin isn't home yet, I was waiting for him," I said.

"Where can he be?"

"With his girl, I guess."

In Berto's home a row of bottles were standing on the side-
board like soldiers on parade.

"What do you have in mind for tonight?" I asked, pointing
to them.

"A good time. All those have to be emptied."

"Then none of us will get home!"

"I've counted on that. You can sleep here."

"I see. Oh, you have Cointreau!" I took the bottle.

"Yes, I got it specially for you!"

"Why!"

"Isn't that your specialty? You'll have to finish it."

"Crazy guy!"

Paul came in with Pierre, the neighbor. They were in high
spirits and danced through the kitchen. I loved listening to Paul's
stories in his beautiful Provençal French. Unlike the Northern
French, he pronounced every syllable, and the way he said his
"r"s was a pleasure to hear.

"Maybe you won't like the Southern dialect," Berto had said
to me once, "it's country French."

The party was in a gay mood; songs were sung and stories
were told. Drinks flowed. At this rate we might yet get through
the supply.

Then Martin came in, looking as I had never seen him; a face
like a thundercloud. He brought wine — as if we didn't have
enough — put his bottles on the table, mumbled something un-
intelligible and sat down with his face in his hands.

"What's the matter?"

He didn't reply but nervously fingered his glass.

"Ah, it's love," Pierre said teasingly. He wanted to make a
joke of it. We all knew that Martin was going to ask formally
for his girl's hand very soon.

"Yes, love!" It sounded like the first clap of thunder in a storm.
He was obviously trying to control himself because of us, though
he was in a mood to have wrecked the whole room. For a moment there was dead silence.

"Come on, have a drink."

He emptied his glass, but the tension remained. The conversations were kept going with difficulty.

"What's the matter with you?" Berto asked.

"It's off," he said, almost inaudibly.

"It's off?" Everybody was tense. They knew what this meant to someone like Martin.

He nodded, but he had to tell more. We were waiting for an explanation.

"I went to her parents this afternoon. They object to the marriage."

Each one felt as if he himself had been rejected.

"Why?" somebody ventured to ask.

Martin became bitter again. "She's from a different class." His girl was the daughter of an executive.

Then, bit by bit, he unburdened his heart. He knew he didn't have to fear making himself ridiculous among his friends, yet his outburst was like a monologue. At that moment we existed for him only as an audience.

"I'm only a worker," he said softly. And with a short, angry movement of his head he went on: "My God, nothing but a worker, a piece of dirt."

Nobody dared say a word; we felt as if we were standing around someone who had just had a fatal accident and was on the point of death. He took his hands from his head and looked at them. He was wet with perspiration. "We're not worth anything because we earn our living with our hands . . ." His monologue continued in a whisper: "I've always done what I could for others. I love her. She loves me." Again he shook his head angrily. "Always that damn injustice, because we're only ordinary people. Always and everywhere the same." It was almost too much for him.

"But Martin," I said, "wait a little longer, maybe they'll change their minds. If she loves you, the decision must be as hard for her as for you."

He looked at me for a moment and shook his head.

"You're a good boy, Frans. . . . All my life I've had to deal with injustice."

"But you've had other things, too."

He showed his hands. Two fingers were missing. Then he let himself go.

"I worked at my uncle's sawmill. I helped him because I couldn't find work and wanted to do something. I worked like all the others there, but got only pocket money. Then I had an accident with the electric saw. Two fingers flew into the air. I saw the boy next to me grow pale as. . . ."

"As an angel," Berto added.

"If I had been an ordinary worker, he would have had to keep me on and pay me compensation. As it was, I just had to leave. I never troubled him about it because I don't want quarrels in the family. Then I came here to the mine. After two years I was fired. You know the story. Now they're hiring people again. I can come back now, if I want to. But I'm damned if I'm going down on my knees for the director."

He was overcome.

"I only kneel for God. I don't go to church, but I am a Catholic and I'll always be one. I believe that I've always been just."

He was unable to go on and cried silently, his head in his arms on the table. A boy as strong as a horse.

After a while he recovered somewhat and felt a little ashamed of himself, but he didn't wipe away his tears.

"Excuse me, but it's too much for me." He got angry again.

"Why all this injustice, even in the Church? Even there you don't count." Then he let go a torrent of words: "I said that I was a Catholic, and I am; I may be even more of a Catholic than all those priests together." He shook his head. "They're living it up and serving their own interests, the Pope in Rome included, and all those other fine gentlemen who are so rich that I don't know how they can justify their wealth before God. . . ."

He was almost frightened by his own words.

"Come come," a few boys said, "don't make it blacker than it is. Not all the clergy are like that. There are good priests, too."

I was very much surprised at this pro-clerical reaction, for none of them practised.

Martin didn't answer. He poured himself some wine to drown his sorrow. More songs were sung and stories told, funny stories

and tragic stories, and Martin did his best to join in. He even
tried to sing a solo with much bravura, but it didn't come off
very well. His mood remained somber.

Toward midnight I tried to leave, but they wouldn't let me go.
Martin was already half drunk.

"Don't be silly, stay here," he said.

"You can sleep all day tomorrow," Berto added.

"All right, but I've had enough to drink."

"We'll make some strong coffee; that'll do us good," Berto
suggested.

"I'm not going to leave." Martin stubbornly shook his head. "I'm
not going to leave. I'm going to undress and lie naked in front
of the door."

"Idiot," Berto said, "you can have a whole bed to yourself."

We drank coffee, but it was too late for Martin. He was
dead drunk.

"Let's go to bed," Berto proposed when it was already far into
the night. He felt sorry for Martin. We helped him get up, and
he was asleep before he was in bed. All we did was take off his
shoes and leave him. Pierre went to his home next door. Paul
and I shared Berto's room and Berto disappeared into his
parents' room.

"Good night," said Paul.

"Good night."

I couldn't sleep late, for I wanted to go to Mass. It was Sunday, the first Sunday I had spent in St. Germain.

When I went to wash in the kitchen Martin was still asleep,
but Berto woke up. Half asleep and much surprised, he brought
me soap and a towel.

"You're up so early, didn't you sleep well?"

"Yes, but it's already eight o'clock."

Paul emerged, too, with a sleepy face. Was he also planning
to go to Mass? I didn't know what time there would be one, but
supposed that until ten o'clock there would certainly be an
opportunity to hear Mass somewhere. We washed. Berto made
coffee.

Paul didn't tell me where he was going so early, and I didn't say anything to him, either. We left at the same time.

I went to the parish church, and was lucky. A Mass was just starting for a handful of people — a few women and some older men. Altogether less than thirty people. The sermon was in Polish. I must have landed among the Poles, who apparently were served from time to time by a priest of their own. But when and where was the Mass said for the parish? I asked the house-keeper when I got home.

"Behind the Salle des Réunions is a room where the priest says Mass on Sunday. But it's a miserable room. The young people never go any more, and it gets worse and worse."

Toward noon Martin came in, a beaten man.

"Hello, how do you feel?"

He mumbled something and sat down listlessly, then beckoned me to come and sit next to him.

"Excuse me for last night," he said softly.

"Oh come on, you just let yourself go. Don't think that I respect you less for it. On the contrary."

"I can't remember anything. What happened finally? I don't even know how I got to bed. I must have been pretty far gone." He ran his hand through his hair with a look of disgust. I smiled without saying anything.

"Frans! . . ." he whispered. "What did I say? Did I say things that weren't just?"

I tapped him on the shoulder. What a child he was!

"When you see that things aren't as black as you thought, you'll be the first to admit it. You're honest enough for that!"

He smiled gratefully.

In the afternoon I suggested that we go for a walk.

"There's a ball in Plasne," he said. "We could go there."

"All right," I said. We wouldn't get that far anyway.

During our walk the conversation turned to the splintering in the ranks of the workers.

"Why do there have to be so many workers' organizations?" he asked. "They only set people against each other!"

"Because no one can serve the people's interests without a certain attitude towards life, and in this everyone differs."

"But why do they have to differ?"

"Well, because not everybody sees matters clearly. You just have to accept that fact. Perhaps even we don't see eye-to-eye on this point."

He looked at me in surprise. "How do you mean?"

"You are a member of the C.G.T.?"

"Yes, I am."

"And what would you say if I were a member of the C.F.T.C.?"

"There you are! What good do they do? They're a splinter party!"

"And what if the C.G.T. operates as a Communist-front organization? Then what should I do if I'm a Catholic? At least the C.F.T.C. is outspokenly Christian!"

"What do you have against Communism? Communism defends the rights of the workers. The Christian party wavers and compromises. That's the difference!"

"And what if Communism is something different from what you think?"

"What do you mean?"

"You only see its surface activity: wage improvement or the defense of such and such a right. But the true character of Communism escapes you."

"What are you saying now?"

"You believe in God, don't you?"

"Yes."

"And you are Catholic?"

"Yes."

"And what if you can't be Catholic and a Communist at the same time, then what?"

"Why couldn't you? Can't you defend the rights of the workers if you are a Catholic?"

"Of course you can."

"Well, then."

"But the struggle of Communism is based on a certain view of life, which neither you nor I can accept. All you see is the struggle."

"I don't follow you."

"For a real Communist only material interests exist. Some spiritual development, too, but only as far as it concerns man's existence in this world. When the Communists have made a paradise out of this world, they have achieved their goal."

"What's wrong with that?"

"In the first place I don't believe that they'll ever achieve it. But furthermore they deny the existence of God and of higher spiritual values."

"What makes you think that? Communism doesn't forbid belief in God at all."

"What that amounts to is that it leaves people alone for a while and tries to win them over by its program alone. It doesn't mention its real aim: to gain territory."

"Then you know more than I do. I've never noticed anything like that."

"But haven't you ever noticed how they speak against the Church and the clergy?"

"Aren't they right in that?"

"Do you believe all they say? The Church is more than they make out, aside from the fact that their propaganda lies and exaggerates."

"And also frankly states the truth."

"Insofar as they do that, I'm for it. But tell me, why are you a Catholic?"

"Because I believe in God and because I was baptized a Catholic."

"And you don't think that religion hinders the progress of society?"

"Why should I?"

"Because Communism does. Where there is belief in God and a hereafter, there is belief in Providence, there is faith and surrender; life in this world is of secondary importance, and want and suffering have meaning. But for Communism the world is all-important. Faith and surrender to God, life with a view to the hereafter, suffering and distress — all this stands in the way of its program. So if the Communist leaders say that religion is opium to the people, this means that they want to eliminate God from society and not in the least that they want to cleanse religion of its incidental shortcomings — which in fact are real shortcomings, since people aren't perfect and don't live the way they should according to their convictions. And although these shortcomings originate with the people themselves, the Communists make it appear as if they were inherent in religion. Suffering and distress are part of our human existence, and not even Communism can get rid of them. Meanwhile any means will serve their purpose to discredit religion. People become Communists for the sake of a program. They don't see any further than that. Yet slowly but surely God is taken out of their lives. Those are their tactics."

Martin had become angry. "Damn it," he said grimly, beating his forehead with his fists. "And it's always the workers who are the victims. How could we know all these things? They always, always make fools out of us." He stamped his feet. "We're nothing but workers, exploited even by our defenders."

Silently we walked on over the slopes to Boudrou. Martin looked for stones to kick at. What an upbringing he must have had, to be so utterly genuine in his reactions!

It was evident a few days later that our conversation had made a deep impression on Martin. A group of railway workers had arrived in our barracks to work in St. Germain for a few weeks. They were old acquaintances of Martin's, since they had been here six months earlier. The reunion was cordial. At night, after we were both in bed, a few of the new arrivals came in to talk. By coincidence the subject of labor organizations came up.

"Well," said Martin, "are you so sure you're not selling your-selves out?"

"What now?"

"There's much more going on than just the carrying out of the program!"

They looked at him questioningly.

"A few days ago I talked about it with my friend over there, a first-class guy." An eloquent gesture made clear that they needn't doubt that I was "square" and reliable. Then he began his explanation.

They listened attentively, then turned to me. So far I had been only listening, but now I had to speak up. They were simple people. The fact that I was a foreigner, recommended by Martin, apparently filled them with respect. They limited themselves to a surprised "Oh" now and then, and nodded signifi-cantly as if to add, "There you are. That's how we're duped." In the end they were clearly disillusioned, and their faces ex-pressed the unspoken question, "What else can we turn to?" But that would have called for another lecture, and it would have been too much for them at that moment. I could do nothing but let them go to bed disillusioned. Providence and reality would do the rest.

16

THE week before I left St. Germain I wanted to pay a visit to the parish priest to compare experiences. Late one afternoon, when it was already dusk, I went to his home and rang the bell.

The door was half opened by a little old woman. I asked if the priest was in.

"What do you want him for?" How many people who had carefully and anxiously prepared their talk with the shepherd of the parish would unburden their hearts to the housekeeper after such a question? To how many such housekeepers would it be a matter of pride to act as guardian angel of the clergy and as intermediary of the faithful? Why doesn't the *Rituale Romanum* provide ordination for clerical housekeepers? Or would a special exorcism be more appropriate?

I ignored her feminine curiosity and answered curtly: "I want to speak to him."

But it wasn't as easy as all that.

"About what?"

With difficulty I remained polite.

"About personal matters!"

Meanwhile I had been observed and weighed.

"The priest has consulting hours in the morning." In other words, if I thought I could do without her, I was mistaken. The door was being shut.

"Excuse me," I said, "doesn't the priest come home at night?"

"He has no time at night."

"In any case I can ask him when he will have time."

"Come back tomorrow morning," was the sharp reply.

"I can't," I replied just as sharply. But I wasn't to underestimate her function.

"Is it important?" she asked.

"That's for the priest to judge."

She could do nothing but capitulate, but she didn't do it without a struggle.

"Why don't you try again in an hour?"

Before turning away I tried to work on her sense of responsibility. "I'll see if I still have time then."

For a moment she hesitated, but before she could offer another suggestion I was gone. She was probably used to simpler callers. "Those miners!"

I walked on for a while, then decided to return to the barracks. I passed the parish house again, and to my surprise the priest was leaning out of the window talking to a farm helper. He nodded cordially. I nodded back but, not wanting to interrupt the conversation, I went around to the front door and rang again.

"I see the priest has come home. Would you ask him if he could see me for a moment?"

Sulkily the housekeeper left me standing in the doorway and went in without a word. I saw the priest shake hands through the window with his parishioner, and a moment later he was standing before me, a young man, as simple and friendly as could be.

I told him my name and said: "Can I have a word with you?" The housekeeper watched in the background.

"Of course, come in!"

He led me to his room.

"You're sure I'm not disturbing you?"

"No, not at all. Sit down."

"First of all, may I introduce myself a little more fully? I am a priest. I've worked here in the mine for a while and before I leave I'd like to compare my experiences with yours."

He was surprised.

"You'll excuse me for not calling on you before," I said. "I thought I'd better not, for it might have caused complications."

"Of course, I understand."

He was a sympathetic man; I knew the workers had nothing against him personally.

"How is the attendance here?" I asked. "I have the impression that there isn't very much."

"Not very much — that's an understatement. Among the workers hardly anyone practises."

"Do the people have their children baptized?"

"Oh yes, all of them. They also get married in the Church

and die with last rites, but that's about all. As long as I've been here, I've only had three cases who refused to have anything to do with the Church even on their deathbed. Two of them were Jehovah's Witnesses and one was a Communist."

"Do you believe that the baptism, marriage and last rites are only family traditions, or is it real faith?"

"What can I tell you? I believe it's more than just tradition, but it's hard for me to judge. The day-to-day religious feeling of the people is something that escapes me. When I have anything to do with them they are friendly enough, but it never goes beyond a nice little talk. Not practising is the most ordinary thing in the world, just as being a Catholic is. If I should try to change that, I wouldn't get very far. The pressure of the community prevents people from being different from one another. The only thing I'd achieve is that they would probably avoid me even more and might not even let me talk to them."

"My personal impression is that there's quite a bit of personal faith involved in this traditional Catholicism," I observed.

"I'm glad to hear that. I really believe so myself, too. But maybe it's just that I want to believe it."

"Aren't you a little afraid of your people?"

"How do you mean?"

"As well as I know the workers, I don't think they deliberately avoid the truth. They're simple people and they're ready for whatever convinces them, whatever seems right to them. But it's hard to convince them of something that has no impact on their lives. The difficulty is to show them how religion can give meaning to their lives. A lot of secondary things will have to be eliminated, but the essence of Catholicism can hold them in such a way that they'll experience it too. They're not unreligious, but they're religious in too much their own way. They want uncomplicated lives, and they feel that the detail of church regulations chokes them. In other words, practising changes life into something God could never have meant, into something that

only people could have thought of; and they're too uneducated
to distinguish between the essential and the unimportant."

"Well, yes . . .," he said sadly. "Have you come across traces
of religion among the miners?"

"Oh yes, even though at first I thought I was dealing with
pagans. They're essentially good people. I love them."

"So do I. But what can I do? I have removed all the traditional
obstacles. I don't take an offering, I don't ask for pew rental—
they don't come, anyway — and with deaths and marriages I
don't even ask for money for a Mass. On those occasions they're
used to having to pay everybody, so they come to settle with
me, too. And when I tell them that all they have to do is pay
for the flowers on the altar, they're surprised and give more.
They're very human, but I don't get anywhere with them."

"I don't understand it," I said. "I've met wonderful boys in
the mine, with a faith that can move mountains. Could nothing
be done through them? When I got to know them, I was surprised that there was no evangelical work of any kind done in
the mine."

"But give me an example."

I told him about Guy, without mentioning his name.

"What?" he exclaimed, surprised and upset. "That happened
in this mine?"

"Yes. Don't be afraid of your people, Father. God is very
close to them."

"I believe you, but usually they say the opposite."

"The tragedy isn't that people reject the truth, but that the
truth doesn't reach them, or they don't understand it."

"How do you think I could reach them?"

"By free booklets in which they could learn about religion as
it affects their daily lives and their problems." I couldn't help
laughing at the idea of this way of solving the problem.

He laughed, too. "Not a bad idea!"

"Or you could let personal conversations grow into small discussion groups, though of course it would take you longer to

reach the masses that way. At any rate I'm not at all pessimistic. I have the impression that God works in a special way in the workers' world, as he does everywhere else in our Christian society. I don't know for sure, but I believe we're living in a wonderful age, a time of return to the original values of life and religion. Sometimes I wonder if I see it that way because subconsciously I want to see it. But the facts overwhelm me."

I said good-bye. The housekeeper didn't know what attitude to take when she saw that insolent fellow walking to the door with his protector. And that after having taken more than an hour of his valuable time!

I had seen Edouard Nilence, the engineer, several times in the mine. He always stopped me and asked how I was getting along. Since the relations between workers and engineers were good, our talks did not attract attention.

The last week I told him I would be leaving soon, and he asked me to dinner on the following Thursday.

On Thursday afternoon I told Martin about it. "I've got to go and see Nilence tonight."

"Well, well, what does he want with you?"

"I don't know. Perhaps he wants to talk about Holland or France."

"He probably wants to talk about the mine."

"I didn't want to say that, but I'm afraid he will, too."

"What are you afraid of? Just tell him what you think."

"I will."

He smiled. He was happy for me and didn't think it strange that I was invited.

"What time are you going?"

"Late afternoon. He's coming to get me. We'll probably take the five o'clock or five-thirty bus."

Noiselessly a shiny black limousine stopped in front of the house.

"There he is," said Martin.

I stood beside him and looked through the window. It was painfully tactless of Nilence to pick me up this way. Another gentleman got out of the car.

"Who's that?" I asked.

"The director-general." Martin bowed to me mock-respectfully. What a to-do! I sat down on the bed, waiting to be called. Martin was still standing at the window, not saying a word. What would he be thinking?

Nervously the housekeeper came to get me.

"See you later," I said to Martin.

He watched me go, smiling. It struck him as extraordinary, too.

The housekeeper went ahead of me to the kitchen, where Edouard introduced me to the director.

"Please sit down," the housekeeper said, busily putting glasses and bottles on the table. It wasn't every day she had such important visitors.

We drank Martinis standing up. Gérard Nilence had told me that the director-general was a saint. He stood there, charming, modest, even retiring. A medieval monk could hardly have had a more spiritual appearance.

We left, with Edouard driving.

"You will have to tell us many things," the director said. "We'll be very grateful to you. You've done important work."

"You must know the workers better than I," I replied.

"No, don't say that. When they deal with us, it's unfortunately from a distance. They're friendly, but they're afraid. They come with their difficulties and grievances, but usually they remain polite and official. No, I think we can learn a lot from you."

I felt that this was not mere courtesy on his part, but genuine interest.

"But you must correct me when you think I don't see things right," I said. "That's important for me, too. And I hope you won't mind if I give you my honest opinion, even when it isn't pleasant. After all, what counts is the truth."

"Yes, yes," he agreed, "don't hesitate to say what you must. We too have our responsibility, as well as you."

Edouard had a tremendous villa with a large garden around it. We drove in through the gate, and just at the moment we came to the front door we had a flat tire.

"Weren't we lucky!" Edouard exclaimed. While we were changing the tire, Edouard's wife and the wife of the director came out to welcome me.

They took us inside, and I saw how richly the house was furnished. We were taken to the drawing room, where aperitifs were served.

The director listened gravely to my story about Filondange. The mine was under his jurisdiction. He didn't really have charge of the one in St. Germain, though he had been its director a few years earlier. My remarks about the human aspects of labor nettled Edouard. He was all in favor of modernization for its own sake, whereas I didn't see the mine as a purely economic institution.

There were a thousand and one things that contributed to the discontent of the workers, I explained. "In a conflict over wages or under certain adverse conditions all these grievances come out at once, and therefore the general dissatisfaction is much greater than the immediate cause of the conflict would warrant.

"On the other hand mechanization makes people more aware of their own importance, as is obvious in the Joy section of the Filondange mine and also in the entire St. Germain mine, but it's fatal when the workers realize that it wasn't done for them but only for the sake of higher production. The work itself may become lighter, but working conditions become inhuman. And when self-assured people become dissatisfied, they're harder to deal with than an anonymous mass."

I went on to say that not enough was done for the cultural development of the workers. In Filondange I had seen how material factors depress and hold down the workers. In St. Germain the workers lived in exceptionally prosperous circumstances. But there it became clear that culture doesn't depend on material things alone.

In St. Germain the workers had nice houses, a lovely village, a modernized mine, a swimming pool, a recreation hall, every bit as good as Paris could offer them. There was hunting, bowling, football, tennis — but what was lacking was the culture of the mind.

"Of course that's the hardest to come by," I admitted. "When you take care of only the material aspects of life, the result is a would-be culture with a certain inevitable arrogance. And I think a worker-priest is in the best position to notice this. The men in Filondange are, I believe, ready for the activities of a worker-priest among them."

I took a breath and continued my story: "The workers in St. Germain aren't, or at least much less so. They would feel insulted if a priest lived and worked as they do. They'd think he felt sorry for them, that he had come to help them, to give them something they lacked.

"But," I said emphatically, "they don't need pity. They're men enough to stand up for themselves when it's necessary, and they don't lack anything they can't get hold of themselves. They don't want the outward trappings of religion, and in fact they might even suspect a worker-priest of condescension. They wouldn't put up with him, or perhaps only after a very long time when they'd realized he wasn't such a bad fellow after all, that he was intelligent and respected them.

"No, what they lack they can get themselves. Boys with lively minds can educate themselves. The only thing is, their religious education will never match their material culture, as things are. For a certain amount of instruction is indispensable.

"Perhaps the solution would be for the boys in the mining school to get not only a technical education but also a cultural one, which shouldn't consist of merely factual knowledge, but should include a concept of life corresponding with their way of living.

"The inclusion of religious education at the mining school and the ensuing regular contact between people and clergy —

using militant and disciplined Catholics — would have to overcome a lot of skepticism. And even if it were accepted some day,
it would be effective only as long as it stayed close to the problems of these people. It would also have to respect individual
responsibility and not degenerate into a spiritual paternalism
which regulated and codified all their activities in detail. Only
then would people be happy in their religion, for the religious
education would have supplemented the religious feeling they
already had.

"We must realize that we are witnessing a return to the
primary values of life and religion. The connection between life
and religion should be explained to people. Thus they would
be able to judge for themselves what is essential and what
secondary. And they must be left to act according to their convictions and their individual sense of responsibility."

The dinner had lasted a long time. The director had been
listening very quietly and thoughtfully. During the conversation
I had insisted: "Please tell me when my observations are incomplete or wrong!" But the reply was always: "It's good for
us to grasp what you're saying. We engineers usually confine
ourselves to our own job, which is a technical one. Too often,
unfortunately, all we do is keep the machines functioning
smoothly and production up to par. We see the workers as a
link in this economic process. And their lives, as far as we're
concerned, go their own way just as our lives do, and whenever
a conflict does crop up we try to solve it by expediency." It was
Edouard who said these things. The director only listened
attentively.

"It would be a good thing if you wrote down all you have
just told us," he said at last. "You would do our workers a great
service, and our engineers would have to take note of it."

"I'd rather wait till I've collected all my experiences," I replied. "I hope to be able to do some good with it, but I'm rather
afraid of publication."

"Why?"

"For one thing, the reality is something so tremendous, that I'm afraid of being unable to give a complete picture of it. I'm happy to be part of it and to see it all around me. But I'm afraid people might take my descriptions for the reality itself, whereas they can only suggest it in a small way. Any description is bound to fall short of the reality. It's too big to be written down.

"So on the one hand I'm conscious of being powerless in face of reality. But it makes me happy at the same time. I'm happy that reality is bigger than I am.

"On the other hand I feel rather helpless because such a great responsibility has been laid on my shoulders, because I'm expected to analyze reality in a way which can be useful. I would prefer it if no one expected more than a simple story of my experiences told to the best of my ability."

"Why not write down what you just told us?" the director said again. "That'll be enough for us."

After dinner we went back to the drawing room for coffee.

"Do you know what suddenly occurs to me?" asked Edouard.

"No."

"The servant girl is from St. Germain. Now she knows you're a priest."

"Then St. Germain will know it too," I said, laughing. "But I'll be ahead of them and tell it myself."

In Filondange I had maintained my incognito to the end. Otherwise they would have informed St. Germain that I was a priest, which would have given me special status. But now there was no longer any reason why I should insist on keeping it a secret. The coal mines where I was now going were a long distance away. And didn't I owe it to the confidence the workers had given me to tell them who I was?

Toward midnight Edouard drove me back to the barracks. Nobody was up. Martin was sleeping the sleep of the just.

After lunch Berto joined us. The three of us were to spend my last afternoon together. We talked about all sorts of things,

but the right moment to tell them about myself didn't come up.
I had to take the initiative.

"Before I leave, there's something I want to tell you. I think
I owe it to you."

"What is it?"

"We're friends, aren't we?"

"I should say so!" Berto said surprised.

"It's bad enough that you're leaving," said Martin, "first Paul
and now you!" Paul had left a few days earlier.

"What I wanted to say is that among friends you really should
know whom you're dealing with, and I haven't yet told you about
myself. I told you I wanted to know the iron mines and after
that the coal mines. I think I know more or less now what
happens in the iron mines, so I'm leaving. I'm going on to the
coal mines to find out about the miners there. But what you
don't know is that I'm a priest."

There was a dead silence. Berto looked at me, speechless.
Martin looked upset—as if I had rebuked him.

"I wanted to find out by experience how the workers live and
what your problems and your needs are," I continued. "I didn't
want to tell you I was a priest until now, because I wanted to be
treated as a worker. I didn't want to study you as an outsider, I
wanted to live the way you do. If I'd said I was a priest, I would
have been in a special position. We might not have become as
good friends as we are now. But it hurt me to have to keep something from you. I believe I didn't deceive you in any way by
using my right to be an ordinary worker among you and become
your friend."

"You're a priest!" Berto finally exclaimed.

"Yes."

"Are you really?"

"Yes, really."

"My God!"

"I hope this won't affect our friendship."

"Why should it, Frans?" asked Berto.

"I don't know, but you have so many objections to the clergy!"
Now the conversation started getting lively. Berto began to
enjoy the whole thing. "Come to think of it," he said teasingly,
"come to think of it, I'm not surprised. Do you remember when
your rosary fell out of your pocket? Of course, it could happen
to anybody, but still, looking back on it . . . . After all, there are
priests who become workers for a while. Not a bad idea, really!"

"I don't understand, Frans," Martin said softly. He shook his
head pensively, as if trying to solve a riddle. "You're a priest?
Really?"

"Yes, I am."

"An ordinary priest?"

"Yes."

"Who says Mass?"

"Yes."

I laughed at his consternation, grabbed him by the shoulders
and shook him a little. "I'm not a ghost, you know."

He had to laugh, too. "No, no, Frans, no."

The next day I said good-bye to the director of the mine.

"I hope you'll tell your impressions to the diocese," he said to
me. "I've always been surprised how many industrial leaders in
France have a genuine concern and feeling of responsibility for
the spiritual needs of the workers. But the question is always
what can actually be done."

In the afternoon I was to leave for Metz. After lunch I said
good-bye to various friends and sat for a while with Martin. Berto
came in too.

Martin was rather solemn. He was sorry I was leaving, but
something else seemed to be bothering him, too.

"What time are you going?"

"I think I'll take the four o'clock bus."

"Oh," he said crossly.

"What's the matter with you? Come with me. We can spend
tomorrow together."

"All right, I'll do that."

Berto said good-bye at the bus stop. He had to play football the next day, otherwise he'd have come, too. "You'll write, won't you?" he called. I nodded.

We sat in the back; no one was sitting immediately in front of us. Martin was still dead serious. It was clear that he had something on his mind. Finally it came out.

"That evening, you remember. . . ."

I knew what he meant.

"I wasn't right, I wasn't fair. . . ."

"I don't know, I think. . . ." I began.

"But I do know," he interrupted me.

"Well, I don't see things as black as you do. But since you spoke out of conviction, you were sincere. Don't worry about it. Suppose everything is as bad as you think, does that mean the Church of Christ is no longer the Church of Christ? You must realize that the Church exists because people are weak and sinful. If people were perfect, they wouldn't need Redemption, and of course they wouldn't need a Church either. The holiness of the Church is in the fact that it preserves God's word in its pure form, and that in it man can meet God in His sacraments, through which he receives God's grace."

We were going over a bumpy road. I could only speak at intervals. Martin just listened.

"The weaknesses of the clergy and of the people shouldn't prevent anyone from meeting God in church. After all, the clergy are people too, and the holiness of the Church doesn't depend on them. The Church is a Church of sinners in that it reconciles sinful people—as individuals and as a society—with God, and it is sacred in that it is Christ among sinful people. Everyone's life is a struggle between good and evil. You mustn't let yourself be upset by that. You and I have the same struggle. But there are enough heroic and holy priests and enough of the faithful to show us the mystery of God's grace in tangible form. If you pay a little more attention to that, your somber picture will change."

He was silent. He didn't speak again until we had been walking through the streets of Metz for several minutes.

"Are you saying Mass tomorrow?"

"Yes."

"Can I be there?"

"Of course, and if you like I'll even say it for you."

"Thank you."

That night we shared a room in a small hotel. He accompanied me to church, made his confession, and for the first time in many years received Communion, which I served him in a side chapel. We were alone together with God. It was hard for me to say good-bye to him and his friends.

Once in a while we still write; not very often. But those letters are dear to me, because my friends and St. Germain come alive in them. They represent a part of my life.

My transfer from the iron mines to the coal mines wasn't without its difficulties. On arrival in France I had found much interest in my work during my week in Arbresle. Several priests had said they were willing to arrange things for me whenever I wanted to work in the coal mines in the North. Before my departure from St. Germain I had written to one of them for detailed information. There seemed to be two difficulties. Because the coal mines, unlike the iron mines, were nationalized, I could be hired only officially, as an apprentice. I had long ago rejected the idea of asking the Dutch government for help in the matter, however.

The second difficulty was that instructions had come from Rome forbidding the French bishops to send out any more worker-priests. Only the existing ones could continue. This had to do with the directive regarding the way these priests were to live which the French bishops had drawn up and sent to Rome for approval. The ban was to be in force for the time it took Rome to study the directive.

Although my case didn't strictly come under these instructions, I could expect to meet with difficulties in my efforts to continue my investigations in the coal mines.

The ensuing complications resulted in my having to give up my plan to go to the North of France. But with the help of Jean Darin I found a new field of endeavor near Lyons.

17

THE day of our departure for the South had arrived. Jean's old Ford stood ready, loaded with baggage. We headed for Nancy. The whole trip would take us two days; the old car couldn't do more than about forty miles per hour.

Jean was a poor man who gave all his energy to research work for various institutions at starvation wages. He never complained and was devoted to his work. He had studied for the priesthood, but failure in his philosophy course had led him back into the world. Strange that one can speak of a man's "returning to the world" after he has abandoned his studies for the priesthood! Now he had a charming wife and two delightful children, Jean Flavien and Marie Antoine. But it was too much to ask of these tots to sit still for hours on end, and we had to buy them some presents to keep them quiet.

It was already dark when we arrived in Jean's home town two days later. Gérard Nilence had told me that it was the most unsavory town he knew; a town of slums. On our arrival I realized that the workers in Filondange and in St. Germain were certainly better housed than my friend Jean.

We stopped in front of an old building, had to climb some stairs and go through a small, narrow archway. There was no light, and we had to grope our way in the dark. At the back of the house were several doors. Outside, also unlighted, was one dirty toilet that served six families. Going through a tiny kitchen we came into Jean's only room. A space on one side, closed off by curtains, served as a bedroom for him and his wife. The children slept on the other side. Jean had only this room to study in, even if the children were making a racket or his wife were receiving visitors.

Jean had told me that he lived very simply and that I would have to rough it the first night, until he could put me up with a friend. I have nothing against roughing it, as long as I'm not in the way, and I cautiously asked if my presence wasn't too much for them. But what could he politely answer except "No, not at all?" When Jean said it, however, it wasn't a mere formality. He had known the situation in advance and would feel hurt if I were to look for a hotel at this late hour.

"You don't mind sleeping over there?" he asked, pointing to the wide couch which served as a bed for the two children.

"No, but what about the kids?"

"They can sleep on the floor," the wife said. "For one night it isn't so bad. We have a spare mattress. Don't worry about it."

The next morning Jean accompanied me to the parish church. What was in store for me? Where would I find work, in the town itself or outside it? In the former case it would be better if I weren't seen saying Mass. We met a priest, a friend of Jean's, and I was introduced. "Oh," the priest said, "you can easily say Mass. The people here are used to worker-priests."

"But I'm not a worker-priest."

"That doesn't matter. Nobody will take any notice of you." I wasn't sure. I knew it would be difficult for me to maintain my incognito in a place where several people knew I was a priest.

While I was putting on the vestments over my windbreaker, I decided at any rate to look for work outside the town.

After the Mass I met the parish priest, an energetic man who had succeeded in bringing some life into his parish. He was very much interested in my work.

"Have you been to see our bishop?"

"No, is that necessary?"

"Necessary?" He looked at me in surprise. "Not necessary, but certainly fitting. He'll be very much interested in what you are doing."

"You don't think he might create difficulties because of the instructions from Rome?"

"Why should he? Yours is quite a different case."

There was nothing to do but go and see the bishop, though I didn't particularly like the idea.

Jean drove me through the town: long, straight streets with big ugly houses, gray and dirty. A mining town. At the outskirts he stopped in front of a big villa surrounded by a garden. This was the home of a manufacturer friend of his, with whom I was to stay. I was surprised. Poverty and wealth got along rather well here.

The manufacturer told me that I could stay with him as long as I wanted, but that finding work wasn't so easy. Jean's children ran excitedly through the big rooms. Jean finally left with them. He asked me to drop in regularly and invited me to have dinner at his Aunt Marie's with the family. I had heard much about Aunt Marie. She was a woman of legendary charm.

My host telephoned the bishop, whom he knew personally. But the bishop was in Lyons and wouldn't be back for at least a week. "Let's call Lyons and see if he can receive me there," I suggested. "I can't sit here doing nothing."

We called Lyons. The bishop himself came to the phone. Of course I should come to see him, he said, he was very much interested in my work. But he couldn't possibly receive me in Lyons, he was busy every minute of every day. He'd see me as soon as he was back. However, I should by all means present myself to the Cardinal in the meantime—he'd find out when it would be convenient. His Eminence's secretary decided: the day after tomorrow at 5 P.M.

I dressed in my Sunday best, but it was a poor outfit. As I had nothing else, the Cardinal would have to receive me that way. I rang the bell at five minutes of five, prepared for the worst. A nun opened the door. I sensed at once that she guarded the Cardinal in the same way the housekeeper in St. Germain had guarded her parish priest.

The Cardinal himself was cordial and full of interest, but because of the new instructions he would not allow me to work in the mines without approval from Rome.

I stayed the night in Lyons and wrote to Rome for permission from the Holy See as well as for money. I was almost without funds. If I'd had to return to Rome, I couldn't have gone because of lack of cash. I mailed the letter and walked around, feeling lonely. I passed a movie theater where they were showing the *Diary of a Country Priest* and on the spur of the moment I bought a ticket.

I thought Bernanos' picture of the young country priest was a little too tragic. If someone could write the diary of the parishioners and see beyond their outward appearance, would it not become clear that God isn't as far from them as this young priest thinks He is? And yet Bernanos gives a slice of reality, a true picture of a priest's depression in face of the indifference of his flock.

If one realizes what Christianity might be and sees what it amounts to in practice, there is every reason to be as depressed as this country priest. But if, on the other hand, one forgot about what Christianity could be ideally and simply tried to find out how much of it was still alive beneath the outward appearance of materialism and sin, then I think one would be surprised at the number of publicans and sinners who would climb a tree in order to see Christ, and who would stand at the back of the church with their hearts full of the prayer "Lord, have mercy on me, a sinner."

How many adulterous men and women would not want to wash Christ's feet with their tears? Man before God, before goodness and love, is everlastingly the same. And perhaps Christ would prefer to live among people like these, even though they don't go to church, and despise His priests. The reverence of these simple people for Christ is startling if one takes into account that they no longer see Him in the priests or meet Him in the sacraments. The tragedy of the priest's life is that among these people Christ goes unrecognized in him, and yet God shows His mercy for them. What is the cause of this seeming powerlessness of the priests?

Why does God allow the priests not to know their flock and the flock not to know its priests? Is it His desire that the barriers that have grown up between them in the course of centuries should be torn down? Is He permitting nature and grace to erupt on a man-made society that has over-conceptualized the essence and working of both nature and grace, thereby sharply separating one from the other? The barriers are cracking everywhere; yet some people cling to them as if their salvation depended on it.

Are "anti-clericalism" and "anti-religion," for example, to be thought of as the work of the devil alone, in both their origin and development? They certainly have something to do with the devil, but there's more to it than that. Could it be that not only can the devil show himself in sheep's clothing, but that grace and nature, too, can have the aspect of a wolf? The brute exterior may hide a reality that is quite different.

We went to dinner at Aunt Marie's. She was a gray-haired lady who still seemed young, who lived very simply on the money she earned as an office worker, and radiated happiness. She had fried chickens as only she could do it. "Monsieur Frans"—that was I— didn't eat nearly enough to please her. I never seem to please my hosts in that respect. And she was mischievous, in spite of her gray hair.

"I can't understand why you became a priest. If you squinted, or were a hunchback, I could understand. But a good-looking boy like you, it's a pity."

Without suspecting it she had voiced an attitude which I've often noticed—namely, that the priesthood is considered almost synonymous with dullness.

18

THE priest of St. Thomas' Church, where I said Mass regularly, had two worker-priests in his care. They worked outside his parish in factories, lived among the people in town, and said their Mass at home. But once every two weeks they came to the parish house for dinner. They were supposed to come the first week I was in town. The priest invited me, too. However, only one of the worker-priests turned up that night. He was a modest man of about thirty-five, dressed as a worker. He was surprised to hear my impressions. He himself was much more pessimistic. Even as a worker-priest he seldom succeeded in giving his people spiritual help. They remained materialist-minded, as if God and religion were unimportant. It took all his resources not to lose courage. It wasn't that he could not talk to them, but that the things that occupied their hearts and minds had nothing to do with religion. Even as a worker-priest he found it difficult to breathe new life into old truths. What could I say against someone with so many years of experience?

I hesitated to tell him my views. I saw the situation differently, but after listening to him I hardly dared believe I was right.

"I don't believe in the atheism of the workers' world," I said.

"We could argue a long time about that. I know some convinced atheists among my worker friends."

"Really?" I asked. "Have you ever let them state their exact beliefs? They can't do it. What does it mean when someone tells a priest: 'I believe in nothing'? About the same as 'Leave me alone.' And to accentuate their antipathy to the clergy, they will ridicule the things a priest stands for, even including God. Does that mean they're atheists? I have never come across an advocate of atheism among the workers. I doubt if even the militant and organized Communists are atheists. And when you pry deeper into the meaning of this 'I believe in nothing,' you'll find every time that they do believe in God after all. At least, that's my experience. It looks as if they live without God or the commandments; they swear and curse like troopers, and they will resist every effort to introduce religious practice into their lives. You can't get them into church, you can't get them to pray regularly, you may not even get them to call a priest when someone is dying. They resist every such effort insolently and blasphemously, or at best indifferently. So the general conclusion is: the workers' world has become paganized. I don't know exactly what percentage of the workers reacts in this way, but I have also found that many workers are much more religious than that."

"But what kind of religious feeling does your first group have, I mean the workers who behave in such a way that they can certainly be classified as atheists?" he asked.

"At heart they're convinced that God is good, and that means they must have great confidence in him."

"But that doesn't get us into Christianity yet!"

"I believe that in our countries, where people still have their children baptized out of tradition—but not without faith—God and Christ mean one and the same thing to the ordinary man. People don't think theologically."

"Maybe, but what's the good of a faith that doesn't affect everyday life?" he asked again.

"I don't know. We're used to measuring people's faith by a list of precepts and prohibitions which they may or may not obey. But it's my impression that this method is too superficial and doesn't take into account the good faith of people who in their ignorance think they aren't offending God, while objectively speaking they are.

"The workers are monotheistic. Belief in secret powers is not the same as polytheism.

"They curse, but I think they hardly know what they are saying. They use their curses more as expressions of strong feelings than as a challenge to God. Sunday is no longer the day of the Lord to them but rather a day of relaxation. They will fight for their day of rest because they're entitled to a holiday, not because of religion. They don't go to church, but they do go to the movies. And if it suits them they'll work on Sundays, too. Is this proof that God isn't real to them in their daily lives? I don't think so. Apart from the fact that they vaguely know that Sunday has something to do with God, they're very ignorant on that point. They may know from tradition that Sunday is the day of the Lord, but they're no longer clear about its meaning. So in that respect they're no longer Christians.

"Love for their parents is spontaneous. Conflicts arise mainly when the parents fail. But usually obligations to parents are met even at the cost of considerable personal sacrifice. You might say they do it to avoid a bad reputation—that is to say, out of human considerations. Meanwhile nature and Christianity as well are satisfied in these demands of society.

"Stealing is not a characteristic of French workers either. Their sense of justice is highly developed, and they would rather help than rob each other. When they do steal, they do so at the expense of the company they work for, and you might call that a kind of earned compensation. They have no intention of harming anyone personally and don't think of it that way.

"They are unchaste, but not generally perverted. They don't commit adultery casually, but they may not think anything of having sexual intercourse with a girl before marriage. Before the children's allowance won acceptance, it was very hard on workers to have children, and they turned to the birth-control practices common in middle-class circles. But the fundamental Christian principle which they do recognize—the prohibition of adultery—is generally adhered to.

"Now you may think that this is nothing but a shadow of Christianity. But on the other hand their respect for God, which includes love, is sincere in spite of their external shortcomings, and they do have a feeling of love for their neighbors. And that, after all, comes close to the essence of Christianity. Moreover, they're generally sincere and simple and open to anything they consider important to their happiness.

"But don't we make the mistake of pointing out their obligations to them the very first chance we get—obligations which have no meaning to them? I think we should start by developing their respect for God and their love for others, and lead them slowly from one step to another. And we should leave it to their own sense of responsibility to act according to their convictions. And these convictions should limit themselves to essential principles of Christianity."

He had been listening attentively, and after some reflection he asked me: "But how are you going to accomplish that? You can't get them to listen to a systematic explanation, and to find the right moment to start a personal religious conversation that begins at the beginning is quite a job."

At my host's I made the acquaintance of an industrialist, a well-educated man and a leading figure in various social research projects. He invited me to accompany him on a business trip to Provence. I had no objections. We would be back within a week, and the letter from Rome might arrive in the meantime.

Early one morning we left in his car. At first we talked about unimportant things. But as we drove over quiet mountain roads, along precipices and through a beautiful countryside he began asking my views on different subjects. We got onto the subject of St. John of the Cross. Wasn't he somewhat alienated from life, and weren't the activities of the clergy often too spiritual? Wasn't it understandable that the Church was unpopular, since it labeled so many things "forbidden"?

"Yet Christianity is very positive," I remarked. "It accepts everything good on this earth. It demands only that the faithful be the possessors of this world in an inner freedom. Every man must surely sense that worldly happiness is unsatisfying even in his moments of joy. But this can't spoil the joy of a good Christian, who knows it is only the reflection of absolute happiness and realizes that in his joy he is 'on the way.'

"The relativity of everything on earth can be compared to the darkness of a night. Just as our eyes cannot fulfill their function in the dark, we cannot fulfill ours in our earthly existence. But there is always the danger that we may lose ourselves in worldly things and suppress our dissatisfaction with the joy of the moment. We must be able to face the fact that everything around us is incomplete; we must have the courage to maintain this relative aspect of all our experiences. This could be called 'active darkness,' and it is not an alienation from life, but on the contrary an acceptance of deepest reality without escape into illusion.

"Only then will man be able to possess everything in love toward God in inner freedom. Life purifies us in part and we must see to the other part—that we don't become slaves of worldly pleasures. Various ascetic methods are based on this, differing according to personalities and circumstances."

"But the usual asceticism can be so oppressive, not to say narrow-minded," my traveling companion interjected.

"Asceticism can only have meaning if it is based on love," I said. "Love of God in those who believe, or love of a certain ideal. In this love all oppression falls away. Only when the level of asceticism is higher than the level of love is there oppression."

We drove past a small river with a newly restored bridge.

"Look, that's the bridge I blew up during the war," my companion said.

"Ha, ha, I didn't know you were such a barbarian."

"It had to be done. The whole town council was against it. It was going to be done at five o'clock in the morning. I had warned the people in the village, so they could decide on which side of the river they wanted to be. Then the council threatened that they would all be on the bridge at five. I told them it was their own business and that they would be responsible for their own suicide. Of course nobody turned up."

He stopped in several small towns for business meetings. It was a lovely trip under a brilliant sky.

As we were to remain in Marseilles for several days I suggested that I go my own way, as my companion was staying at his father-in-law's. I wanted to see what the worker-priests did and, if possible, stay with them.

The harbor district in Marseilles looks poor. After some searching I found the house where the worker-priests lived. In one of the streets was a big church; I figured it couldn't be far from there. The church was about fifty years old, and next to it stood a solidly built house which I took to be the parish house. But it turned out that no priests were living there any more: they had gone to live among the people.

Diagonally across from the church was a slum. That's where I was told to go. The slum row led to a small open space, surrounded on three sides by houses and on the fourth by a wall with a hole in it through which you could get into another street. The one-story, barracks-like houses gave the impression of having been put up by the inhabitants themselves. They looked makeshift and dilapidated. Father Loew was supposed to be living somewhere near. I asked around. Father Loew? Oh yes, Jacques and Max did live there, but they weren't home.

The place where the Fathers lived was a crude stone house with an unpainted double door that was two-thirds cut-glass panes. Through it a kind of workshop could be seen. I looked in vain for a bell, but someone inside had noticed me and opened the door. I might have just gone in. The young man who opened the door for me was a worker, but there was something about him that indicated a different background.

"Does Father Loew live here?" I asked.

"Yes, but he's out working at the moment. So is Father Max. Can I help you?"

I introduced myself as a priest.

"I'm still a seminary student, working here as an apprentice for a few months," he said.

"Would it be possible for me to stay here for a few days?"

"Oh yes, of course. There's room for three men, and one of the Fathers just left. I don't sleep here. I go to the vestry at the back of the church. Make yourself at home. Father Max will be home around five. I'll tell him about you. I have to leave in a few minutes."

We walked through a middle room where there was a telephone, and from there he led me to the combined bedroom and study of the priests. It contained three unpainted tables loaded with papers and books, and three beds as shabby as any I'd ever seen. The bedding looked like nothing but bunches of old rags. The room was low, like the rest of the house. Book shelves covered most of the wall space. It didn't take me long to see that their library was up to date.

"Make yourself comfortable. Perhaps you'll find something to read until they come home," the young man said.

"Thanks. I'll find something to do. I have some papers to write, anyway."

"Fine. We'll see each other again later."

He left.

I thought it would be rather too forward of me to stay in the room with all those papers, so I went back to the first room in back of the glass door, where there was a long wooden table with some chairs, a sink and a stove. I sat down and started to write. Some street boys looked through the glass, came in, looked me over and asked: "Who are you?" as if I'd entered their home without permission. I smiled at them but said nothing. They came and stood next to me.

"What are you doing?"

"Writing."

"Isn't Max here?"

"No."

"Oh." They disappeared again.

A woman came in. She greeted me, and without another word went to the middle room to make a telephone call.

A young man came in and asked: "Is Max here?"

"No."

"Where is he?"

"I don't know."

"Oh." He walked out.

Two other young men came in to telephone. All they said was "*Bonjour.*" It went on like that. People kept coming in to make phone calls. Finally I moved to the other room after all. But there, too, people came in and asked for Max.

At last Max arrived. We introduced ourselves. Of course I could stay, he said. Wasn't I hungry? He casually looked through some papers and acted as if I'd been living with them for a long time. He was about thirty-five, with an intelligent face and quiet movements.

"Father Loew will be home at six. He works at the docks. I work here in the neighborhood so as to be on hand if anything happens."

Some men came in. "Max, come along, will you? We're fixing some electric wiring and we can't finish it in time." Max went.

At about six Father Loew came in. They called him Jacques. He looked about forty-five. He hurriedly drank a glass of milk and excused himself for having to leave again right away.

"You're very welcome. Only we can't offer you very much. I'll show you where you can sleep." He went ahead of me to the middle room. "You won't see much of us, but I hope we'll find a few minutes now and then to talk. There's Mass at seven o'clock, and before that I have to make several calls. Just make yourself at home and do as you please."

"Can you keep it up, running around all day like that?" I asked.

"Oh yes, why not? Our work is fairly simple. We share the lives of the people around us and hope to be a living evidence of Christ in their midst. See you later." He disappeared.

I saw that I couldn't do much more in those few days than watch.

At seven o'clock I went across the street to Mass. It was already dark. I was the only one entering the church, and I expected it to be almost empty, as it was an ordinary weekday. I was surprised to find the contrary. The church was well filled with all kinds of people, men and women, boys and girls. Up front a new table altar had been put in front of the old altar; it was here that the priest was to say Mass, facing the crowd. The walls were painted with scenes from the lives of workers. It was very quiet. The people were waiting respectfully for the arrival of the priest. I was impressed by this unusual spectacle in the poor quarters of Marseilles on a weekday, and I stayed in the back of the church.

A few minutes later Father Loew entered quietly, dressed in a white Gothic chasuble. He was alone, without an acolyte. There were plenty of boys and young men in the church, but nobody got up to help him. Should I go? I decided to wait awhile. He prepared the chalice for the Mass according to the Dominican rite. Still no acolyte appeared. I thought I'd better serve him, so I went up and knelt behind him, also facing the people. But instead of beginning with the prayers at the foot of the altar, he first made a short speech about the saint whose day it was. He spoke from the heart to a community of friends and fellow workers, and his words were full of wisdom. (He did this every day.)

I waited patiently on my knees for him to finish. And suddenly he ended with: "And finally I am happy to welcome a guest in our midst, who will stay with us for a few days. He is a priest-professor from Rome, who also lives as a worker as often as he can." I was startled. What had prompted him to say that?

Finally the Mass began. I now saw that I was completely superfluous as an acolyte, for the Dialogue Mass was said in French, and the whole church answered. No conducting for rhythm was necessary, the prayers were not said hesitantly, as if they were unfamiliar. It was a living community around a mys-

tery that was about to occur. How powerfully moving these short,
fervent responses became! I felt as if I were at a meeting of the
first Christians, as if I were spiritually baptized again. It was
impossible to escape the overwhelming impressiveness of the
occasion. The priest, who was one of the people, who was called
Jacques by everyone, kissed the altar, silently prayed the Introitus
to himself and said with urgency in his voice: *"Dieu, Père, ayez
pitié de nous."* The answer didn't come solemnly as a part learnt
by heart, but as a real cry of the people, *"Dieu, Père, ayez pitié
de nous."*

Dieu, Fils, ayez pitié de nous . . . Dieu, Fils, ayez pitié de nous.
*Dieu, Esprit d'amour, ayez pitié de nous . . . Dieu, Esprit
d'amour, ayez pitié de nous.*

The Gloria was prayed together. Jacques—what else can I call
him?—had nothing theatrical about him. His movements were
precise and controlled. With the gesture of one bestowing a gift
he said earnestly: "May the Lord Jesus be with you." And his
friends said the same for him.

It continued like that. Only the Offertory and the Canon were
prayed in silence. The only thing I had to do was to give the
ampulla. Almost everyone went to Communion after saying the
confiteor together.

What was I to think of all this? Was there a spiritual revival
taking place in this rough workers' district that could put many
an old and godly parish to shame? Or was this, too, a piety confined to the church, a small oasis of spiritual life unrelated to
the rest of the day? I could hardly believe that. These people
must at least have the conviction and courage to sustain themselves during the day, to be able to receive the Body of Christ so
devoutly during the Mass.

I expressed my surprise to Father Loew about what I had seen.

"We can be grateful to God, but you mustn't have any illu-
sions," was his reply. "These people are only a very small part of
our parish. Even on Sundays we get less than ten per cent of the
population."

"All right, but this little group seems to be of an unusual caliber."

He smiled. I was soon to find out how high were his standards for the practice of Christianity.

"Why did you tell these people who I am?" I asked.

"I try to avoid as much as possible giving our people the impression that we are a different kind of priest. We enjoy their confidence and affection because we live and work as they do. We belong to their community. That's why I had to explain what kind of a person you are. I did it publicly in order to dispel any mistaken ideas. These people are inclined to think that the other priests, the bishops and Rome are on the side of the middle class and of capital. That's why I take every occasion to show this is not true."

Max prepared the dinner. We ate together. I saw that the private life of these priests was reduced to a minimum. Anyone who felt like it could come in without knocking for a chat. And if someone wanted to see one of the priests personally, the two of them would disappear into the telephone room. There was a continuous coming and going. They even sat with us at the table. We had some roasted chestnuts, and whoever came in got some, too. One of the fellows had a cantaloupe at home. He went to get it, and shared it with us. We smoked each other's cigarettes. In short, this was community life on a large scale. An old woman came in to ask for a Mass to be said. The request was written down as well as the hour on which the Mass was to be said. No fee was asked. There was no pew rental, and at marriages and burials no contributions were asked for. The priests lived on what they earned themselves. The whole neighborhood could use the telephone. There was only a notice on the wall that people had to pay for their own calls and put the money in a box next to the phone. No one ever took advantage of it: the exact amount to pay the bill was always there. Anyone could walk in all day, even when nobody was home. Nothing was ever stolen.

The priests had their hands full. They had made a piece of land, the property of the church, available for housing construction. The houses were put up by the people themselves, and the priests helped whenever possible. Gradually Christianity had become an authentic reality to these people. A reality growing out of life itself. Jacques and Max were people just like themselves; only they had a spiritual authority which had grown spontaneously and was rooted in the community.

The first to join us at dinner after Mass that first evening was a man of about forty. He had been very much disturbed by a retreat in which he had participated not long before. He was in despair at being such a great sinner. Every day he harped on the same theme. Apparently there was a priest in Marseilles who organized retreats for small groups of workers. I heard that Jacques and Max didn't like the idea, because he upset people with his thundering sermons.

The man's laments were interrupted by the arrival of Gines and his wife. Gines was a laughing Spaniard with the heart of a child and an I.Q. of probably no more than ninety. They had arrived a short time ago and had nowhere to turn. The priests had given them a room in the tower of the church. Now they were satisfied and happy, and considered themselves part of the family. I should write to him, Gines said to me. Of course I would write to him. People appreciate some kind of sympathy from others, even if they are hardly acquainted.

19

AFTER some days my traveling companion came to pick me up for the return trip. He had stayed in Marseilles longer than I had anticipated.

We drove along the coastal lakes of the Mediterranean via Arles to Nîmes. There had been a lot of rain, and we had to make a detour because one of the roads was under water. We talked about social problems.

"Do you know what I think is so strange?" he said.

"No. What?"

"I know an institution that studies social justice and fights Communism, and all the while it is up to its ears in debt so that it can't carry out its obligations to the people who invested money in it. That's number one. Furthermore they were offered a million the other day and they accepted. That's number two. I think both things are against the justice they fight for."

"The first thing may be unjust. I can't judge that right away. But why should the second thing be against justice?"

"If you fight capitalism, you shouldn't accept money from capitalism," he stated flatly.

"I don't quite understand. Do you consider capitalism unjust in itself?"

"Yes, of course, don't you?"

"I think capital is unjust only when it has been acquired by unjust means. The social struggle is, after all, more against the exploitation of the workers than against capital as such."

"I wonder if capital can ever be acquired by just means. It is accumulated in the first place either by financial speculation or by profiting from the labor of others, and even speculation is based on exploitation."

"But don't you profit from the labor of your workers?" I asked. "You drive a car, they don't. Aren't you tied to a nationally regulated wage level?"

"The injustice is regulated socially."

"I think that's true to a large extent. But meanwhile everyone has the right to possess the fruits of his labor. To me this is the right to have capital. If everyone had to start from scratch, not many would ever acquire large capital. But capital has also grown historically and is handed down from father to son. Am I responsible for the origin of the capital I inherited or received some other way? Supposing I am, and you apply the principle that the receiver is as bad as the thief: even then I won't be able to make up for any injustice done before my time. But I *will* be able to spend the money in the public interest. So I should say that a social institution can receive a gift of a million without any qualm about compromising with injustice."

It was dark by the time our business in Nîmes was finished. We wanted to cross the Rhône near Orange, but the bridge had been destroyed during the war and was not yet rebuilt. We had to cross by ferry. Under the light of the moon we admired one of the most beautiful Roman aqueducts in France, and by the next evening we were back home.

No word from Rome. No report as to how matters stood or whether I would have to wait a long time, and no money. My host lent me some. But I didn't want to take advantage of his hospitality for weeks on end, even though he assured me I could stay as long as I wanted.

I thought the best thing to do was to go back in the direction of Marseilles and visit Paul, the apprentice from St. Germain. I stayed in the neighborhood of Marseilles and Toulon for about a week. A young lawyer offered me a ride back as far as Avignon, where I would have to turn off in a different direction. We talked about the Back to Nature movement, of which he was an advocate.

"Don't you think this movement encourages sexual liberties?" I asked. He looked at me surprised. "I don't think so. The people I know personally in the movement are very high-minded."

"Do you believe these practices can be reconciled with Christianity?"

That question was a leap in the dark. I didn't even know to what faith my companion belonged.

Again he looked at me in surprise. "Don't ask me. I don't have

any religion. I believe everybody should decide for himself how
he wants to live. In naturalism I see a free way of life."

"What you call a free way others may call libertinism."

This irritated him somewhat. "What libertinism? Do you think
only religion can give you principles? I think the opposite is true.
The closer you are to nature, the more respect you get for life."

"Then do you consider religion unnatural?"

"Religion? Religion is something archaic, something that's outside life. It has nothing to do with God. It's just like the performance of a symphony by Beethoven. A swanky concert hall with
plush, musty seats and the coughing and sneezing of the elegant
audience. A place like that makes it impossible to play, or at least
enjoy Beethoven properly. It's the same with religion. It has much
that is venerable, but it's all old, musty, dusty and messy."

So he saw religion merely as going to church.

"No," he continued, "that has nothing to do with life or with
God. And add to that the selfish politics of the clergy—no, I like
life lived honestly. As far as that goes, I think the Italians are the
most sympathetic in their religion. They are less formal, more
free. And when they confess, they do it properly."

I felt like asking if he had ever heard a confession but I held
my peace.

"The value of anything depends on the way you do it," he went
on. "And you have to stand up for your principles and your
actions. You have to admit your mistakes, too, and not try to cover
them up. That's cowardly."

By this time we were driving through bare, blue mountains.
"Do you believe in any special religion?" he asked suddenly.

"Yes, I am a Catholic."

"Oh," he said in a tone as if he felt sorry for me.

From Avignon I went on by bus to Rovin where Paul, the
apprentice from St. Germain, was studying. It was raining when
I arrived late at night. I had left the fair weather behind me on
the Mediterranean. I saw Paul the next morning. He was back at
the mining school, without the prestige he had enjoyed as an

apprentice—but he had never cared much about that. We were happy to see each other again. I wanted to tell him I was a priest: he would hear it anyway in St. Germain and might feel hurt if I hadn't told him personally.

So I told him on the way to a bar, and said our mutual friends knew, too.

"Damn it, Frans . . . ." He laughed. "What did Martin say?"

"The first moment, just about what you said. He couldn't get over it. But we remained good friends anyway."

Paul and I, too, went on talking like old friends, as if nothing had happened.

A week after my departure I was back at my host's in St. Etienne. Still no word from Rome. I couldn't understand it. Why didn't they tell me at least how matters stood? How much longer would I have to wait? I told the priest of St. Thomas', who was sorry he had put me in such an uncomfortable situation, that I felt like visiting the various mines in the neighborhood, to get an over-all picture. After all, whether I visited the sights in town or the mines couldn't make any difference. He agreed. I asked if he knew of a place to stay in town. I didn't want to take any further advantage of my host's hospitality. Yes, he did know of a place.

The director-general of the mines in Varel and the surrounding area was a cousin of the priest's. He surely could arrange for me to visit the mines. The priest wrote an introduction on a visiting card, and with that I went to Varel, about three quarters of an hour by bus from St. Etienne. The administration building of the mine was big and the atmosphere official. When I asked to speak to the director-general, the doorman said this could be done by appointment only. I gave him the visiting card, asked him to show it to the director, and said I would wait for the reply. When he returned he asked me to follow him. He took me to a waiting room, from which I would be called. The director was in conference, but I didn't have to wait long.

I told the director, who was a serious, businesslike man, that I was a priest and would like to work incognito and if possible, live among the workers to become acquainted with their spiritual problems.

"Of course you can work here," he replied. "But it will be difficult to hire you officially as a miner, for that would involve workers' organizations and contracts. The only thing is to take you on as an apprentice, as they did in the iron mines. But the coal mines are nationalized, and as you can only be hired unofficially, I don't see how I can pay you an apprentice wage."

"If it's impossible, I'll do it without pay."

"I can't put you up. That's a big problem here. Do you have a place to stay in town?"

"Yes, I have."

"Then I'll inform the mine administrator in Plouvy of your arrival. Go there tomorrow to arrange everything. The mines in Varel are not quite suitable." (Why? I wondered.) "Besides, Plouvy is closer to town. You can commute by bus."

I said good-bye to my host and left for my new quarters. My mail would continue to be sent to him, so I should not be out of reach. I was now an ordinary lodger and would have to do my own shopping. I wasn't exactly used to that. Only once a day could I get a hot meal from my landlady.

20

THE management at Plouvy was extremely courteous. There were three mines: one in Trasny, one in Donal and one in Rochy. They ran in different directions and at various depths, but all were served from one installation above ground. I said I had to limit myself to visiting for the time being, as I might be called away from France at any moment, but that I hoped I'd soon be able to work in the mines.

I got a worker's pass for the bus, and as soon as I knew I could stay, I could have one of the apprentice's rooms at the mine dormitory. I was to report the next day.

Since I would have to take the 5:30 bus from St. Etienne every morning and wouldn't have time to say Mass, I asked the priest of the St. Thomas's church whether I could do it at night. He thought I was entitled to the privilege of a worker-priest, and we agreed on 7 P.M. as a suitable hour. It took place in total silence, I without even an acolyte, all by myself in a big empty church.

In the early morning I had to heat coffee, make my lunch, swallow a piece of bread and run for the bus, often through rain and wind. "That's life," as they would say in Filondange. I was back in the swing of it.

The number of workers going by bus to Plouvy was not very large. I didn't know them, and they always got out at the stop before mine. I walked to the mine by myself. At that early hour it was still pitch-dark, but the picture of the mine was all the more fascinating. It was a large installation with high and low, red and white lights, shunting trains, white clouds of steam over the fiery glow of the coke that was being cooled, a magic city in itself, a mysterious expression of the story of labor.

Dwarfed by my surroundings I walked past high chimney stacks, coolers, semaphores, connecting bridges, as through a machine that was never still, in which the people went round and round with the wheels. In the monasteries at that moment my brothers in religion were closing their meditation books in order to begin Prime. Two entirely different worlds.

As day came this fairy tale of the mine turned to grim, grimy reality. A reality not without its poetry, but a poetry of distress trapped in continuous drudgery—an imprisonment from which everyone wants to escape, but to which everyone must be resigned.

I visited the mines all morning, and at two in the afternoon I came to the surface, so black with dirt that I had to wash three times before I was presentable. Then back to town.

Fortunately I wouldn't have to go back and forth much longer. I now got an affirmative answer from Rome. Permission had been given as soon as I applied, but the letter had been sent to the wrong address, then remained at the post office for some time before it was sent back as undeliverable. So the mystery was solved. The letter was a *"permesso di continuare, per ragioni particolari di studio, a rimanere, vestito da secolare, in mezzo agli operai di alcune officine della Francia. Attese le speciali circonstanze del caso, questa Suprema S. Congregazione concede il richiesto permesso "ad duos menses."*

The time limit of two months was sufficient. It's the custom in Rome to grant permission of this kind for only two months, and then extend it.

I sent one of the two copies I had received to the Cardinal, asking him at the same time for official permission to say Mass at night. Meanwhile I continued to live in St. Etienne, because I thought it wasn't a good idea to say Mass in Plouvy itself. But my commuting was to be over soon. The Cardinal replied that in accordance with the permission from Rome he would allow me to work in his dioceses. He asked me to write a short report of my experiences before leaving, and finally expressed his regret that he couldn't grant my request to say Mass at night. He could only grant this to the worker-priests of his own area, and I wasn't one of them.

During my visiting days in Plouvy I had received every courtesy and respect from the management and the engineers. Now that I was an ordinary worker I was to escape this special treatment only to some extent.

As a visitor I had been given high boots, a headlamp, woolen trousers and a wool shirt, and I had used the shower rooms of

the management. All this remained unchanged when I started
work as a miner, and I couldn't get anybody to understand why
I wanted to be treated like everyone else.

The three mines that came together at the large pithead above
ground stretched out in different directions and at different levels.
First I had visited the old Trasny mine with one of the engineers.
The shaft was still operated by a steam engine, and the elevator
was not meant to carry people. The roof was so low that we had
to crouch. The floor and the walls were covered with a thick
layer of dirt, and there was a steady drip of water from the roof.
The workers in this mine usually took the elevator of the adjoin-
ing mine which was connected with Trasny, or descended on foot
through a corridor which started above ground and went down
gradually. On the days I visited the mine it was mostly empty.
Only here and there did we come across small groups of miners
who worked bare-chested, and usually in short pants. Some of
them wore enamel medals of the Virgin Mary around their necks.
They kept a friendly silence toward the engineer.

Th main corridors were narrow and low. Hardly ever could I
walk upright. There wasn't much to see, anyway.

Another engineer took me to the mine in Donal. The elevator
roof leaked there, too, but at least we could stand upright. After
having walked around with him for a few days, I asked him to
let me work there.

A few days later I went down with the group I had been assigned to. The men didn't wear special working clothes, just some
old rags. Silently we went through the corridors to the place of
work, a walk of about twenty minutes. Then we came to a hole
about a yard high, through which we had to crawl into another
corridor which narrowed as we went along. After a while we
couldn't crawl any more, and had to pull or push ourselves forward, lying flat on the floor. We went on that way to the end.
The corridor was so narrow that it was impossible to move either
left or right. After this effort we finally arrived in our *chantier*.
In a bent-over position we had to move along a path about twenty

inches wide that ran between the shoring timbers alongside the conveyor-belt and the wall out of which the coal was cut. You could also throw yourself on the conveyor-belt and have yourself taken to your destination lying face down. But of course this involved taking hold of one of the side supports at the right moment and jumping with agility.

In the *chantier* it was warm, but bearable. Everyone undressed to his shorts. The foreman explained to me how to measure the gas content of the air with an ordinary, non-electric lamp, and what the danger point was. But in this corridor the threat of gas wasn't very great.

It was much hotter than in the iron mines, but the work was much lighter. The layer of coal wasn't particularly hard. Even I could handle a drill without difficulty. The wall could be cut like cake, and there was no danger of heavy chunks falling. While my co-worker put up the supports—a thing I couldn't do—I drilled. It was also my job to see that the coal got onto the conveyor-belt. After a short while we were pitch-black.

A little further along, where the corridor was sloping and where it was only possible to work squatting or kneeling, a few miners were having difficulty in putting up props. They needed help. The swimming trunks of one of them were so worn that they ripped with the strain. He took them off and went on working beside me, stark naked. No one paid any attention to it. He worked that way all morning. Everyone had enough to do, anyway. Little was said, and during the lunch break they talked only about everyday things or about a football match. The conversations were not banal, nor were they about politics—still less about religion. I had noticed in the iron mines, too, that generally speaking the conversations were not banal and even if they were, they were not typical of the miners' mentality. Vulgar topics were usually introduced only by a few undesirables who happened to be present.

One day they discussed schools. Everyone agreed that parochial schools were better than public schools. It used to be quite dif-

ferent, they said. Even those who apparently had little use for the
Church, and whose children went to public schools, listened with
interest and asked how they could get their children into Catholic
schools. When I asked what the difference was they couldn't
really tell me. In the workers' world a statement is often accepted
as truth as long as no one challenges it, and in this case no one
openly disliked the activities of priests and other religious people.
They explained to me that religion was taught in those schools
and they thought it was a good thing. And when I asked in surprise "They teach religion?" they apparently thought I was a
heathen and explained helpfully: "Yes, that's the doctrine of
Jesus." They were quite serious and regretted it if they couldn't
get their children into the Catholic schools.

I also worked in a different section of Donal. To get there we
couldn't use the elevator at all. We had to walk about half an
hour from the pit-head. Over my wool shirt I had nothing but a
thin jacket, and the weather was cold. When it rained there was
no alternative but to arrive wet. There was a small building
against the slope of a field from which a corridor led to the mine.
At the entrance my glasses always got steamed, and I couldn't
go on until they were clear again. There were no stairs going
down; we had to hold on to a cable so as not to slide down more
than a hundred yards over the slippery earth, and grope our way
downward with our lamps as the only illumination. Water kept
dripping on us.

At the bottom of this steep corridor we landed in water and
had to wade through it in order to get to the swinging doors of
the mine itself. The main corridor was narrow. Whenever dump-
carts passed we had to press ourselves against the wall. But the
best was yet to come. Through an opening in the wall we suddenly found ourselves in front of a precipice. Here, too, our own
lamps provided the only illumination. From there we had to get
down to the bottom. Some old railway tracks had been fastened
to the wall, and we had to descend vertically along the ties. But
in some places the ties were missing, and we had to let ourselves

down by sliding along the tracks, groping in the dark. Going back up we needed the help of the rough rock wall as well. Once we had arrived at the bottom after this neckbreaking feat, we soon came to the place of work. Here, too, was a conveyor-belt, and the job was the same as in the section I had worked previously. It was not as hot, but we worked in shorts anyway as the rest of our clothes usually got wet during the trip down.

I first worked with a young Frenchman whose whole joy in life was his motorcycle, and later with a Yugoslav who had fled because he would have no part of Communism. He was of peasant stock and loved to treat me to ham and wine in the afternoon. His greatest joys were work and freedom. He didn't worry about anything else.

I made friends with a Pole who was married and lived in Plouvy. He often took me home with him. His constant complaint was that they still had to go and get their water at the end of the street. Many times we played table tennis in the village. Politics and religion played only a small part in the lives of these people. In spite of the rather primitive conditions in which they worked, they managed to be friendly. What kind of endurance or adaptability enabled them to remain good-natured under those circumstances? Or was it not a question of virtue but only of dull resignation? Or perhaps a mixture of both?

21

Though I had been in Plouvy for some time, I had never been taken to the mine in Rochy. But the chief engineer was a very sympathetic man and willing to grant my every wish. I saw him almost daily, and he would often have maps drawn for me of the parts of the mine I had visited. When I asked him one day whether I could go to Rochy, he replied that the work there was very hard indeed, but that I could go with one of the engineers if I insisted. The engineer only showed me a layer of coal between Donal and Rochy which lay deeper than the rest.

"You'll have to do some gymnastics," he warned me when we set off.

He hadn't exaggerated. We arrived in a layer of coal that went down in a slope extending over more than three hundred yards. We couldn't walk or even crawl down, but had to slide over the slate-like earth. And we went fast, for it was steep. Above and beside us were timbers which we could grab at any time. Try sliding down a slope of hard, uneven stone with nothing on but a shirt and pants into which the coal grit penetrates! After about a hundred yards it became unbearable. Sometimes the grade leveled off for a few yards. In those places there was usually water. As it was impossible to go around it, we had to shove ourselves, prone, through the water, and then we began to slide again at high speed. I'd never realized that it took so much human effort to stoke our stoves!

Alongside us as we slid down, some miners were at work, kneeling or squatting. But this was only a tour of inspection.

"Is this Rochy?" I asked when we finally landed in a corridor.

"No, Rochy only starts here. But this is enough for today." I agreed.

"Do miners have to go to work like that every day?" I asked. The descent alone would be about a day's work!

"Oh, no," my companion said smiling, "they go by elevator." Visitors never came here, nor to Rochy itself.

"Well?" the chief engineer inquired when I returned.

"That was quite something!" I said.

He was amused. "And what next?"

"Let me work in Rochy. I know the people in Donal now more or less."

"Can you face it?"

"What do you mean?"

"We have a lot of trouble with the people in Rochy. They're outspoken Reds."

"I don't mind."

He took me to the foreman of the shift that had just come back from Rochy, and it was arranged that I should go with him early the next morning.

The shaft of Rochy lay some distance from the pit-head. When I arrived a group of workers were already waiting to go down. Little was said. Some of the men glanced at me indifferently: a newcomer. They were a different type of people from those in Donal. But different in what respect? They looked rougher to me, more impudent, more uncouth even. Yet they didn't act that way. In other mines you could see the difference between workers in the mechanized and non-mechanized sections of the mine. But what was the difference between Rochy and Donal? All I knew was that there was a lot of dust and heat. Would that turn people Communist?

The foreman let all the miners go down first, before he and some other foremen got into the elevator. Few of the men had electric headlamps; most of them had hand lamps. We arrived in the mine. The foreman wanted to take me along on his trip through the various sections, and after that I could start work.

It was quite a walk. In the beginning I didn't notice the heat particularly. But after the last swinging doors it really became very warm. Anyone working in this temperature would soon be hot. The foreman took off his shirt. It surprised me somewhat, for I'd never seen a foreman do that. They always remained dressed, even when the miners worked half naked.

"It's going to get hot!" He indicated that I should follow his example.

We went on and checked a ventilating station. But I couldn't tell where the fresh air was supposed to be, for all the air seemed thick and muggy. As in the warmer sections of Donal, workers wore only shorts. We walked through a high, brightly-lighted corridor where some men were busy shunting dump-carts. A few of them walked along with us for further instructions. The corridor was being lengthened. The workers listened to the foreman attentively and without any sign of resentment. They had no immediate cause for resentment anyway, as far as I could see.

A young man approached, stark naked. He wore just a belt around his hips, to which the battery of his headlamp was attached. Nobody objected to his walking around like that. He joined us, and he turned out to be a technician. There seemed to be trouble somewhere, and a long discussion between him and the foreman followed. The naked youth talked at length, led the way to some hard-to-reach spots and climbed to various points to show what could and what couldn't be done. A curious guide.

We went back to the ventilating station, where they talked some more. It took a long time, but finally we continued our trip. It was quiet in the corridors.

We crawled through a hole and came to a cave where some Moroccans were having their lunch. Quiet people who gave us a friendly greeting. Now it was getting dark. We were approaching our destination. Only here and there was a light, the air was muggier and filled with black dust. We passed an old miner who was drilling. He was completely nude. The foreman asked how things were going. A long row of lights indicated where drilling was in progress. The noise was deafening and the heat terrible. We kept passing naked workers.

"It's pretty hot here," I remarked.

"Just wait, we aren't there yet."

We crawled through another hole and arrived at the upper end of a slope. Drills were roaring, a shaker conveyor rumbled, and through it all the ventilator was humming like the string section in an orchestra. The noise was overpowering. The illumination was better than in the other section, but the close, black mist was so thick that I couldn't see more than five yards in front of me.

"The vein of coal is very, very hard here. That's why there is so much dust," the foreman explained. It was as if we had arrived at the core of hell. No wonder the workers were stripped.

Even without working we perspired over our whole bodies and got pitch-black. There wasn't much space between the shaker conveyor and the wall, and it was almost impossible to stand upright. In this narrow space black, sweating, naked men were crawling alongside me. Others thundered their pneumatic drills into the layer of coal. They were so heavily coated with soot that the perspiration pouring down their bodies didn't even leave white traces. With their shiny black bodies they looked like devils. But they were devils that didn't differ greatly from me, for they had friendly smiles which showed their white teeth when we talked to them. The white of their eyes contrasted brilliantly with their dark faces. And their lips were blood-red.

They had to work under extremely hazardous conditions. The ghost of silicosis was always with them. They felt the heat in their sweating bodies and the fatigue in their trembling muscles. They couldn't see themselves as an artist would. Never had I seen the struggle of man against nature so dramatically portrayed. Never, either, had I seen the beauty of the human body take on such impressive proportions—the more so as the men themselves weren't aware of this beauty. It was nature against nature—under conditions which would make a humane sociologist's hair stand on end.

You might also say they were slaves. But slaves that were kings of nature. Strong, muscular fellows in shining black nudity.

The foreman left me with a quiet, friendly boy who needed a helper. I had to get the coal onto the shaker conveyor. The wall gave way to my naked partner. With tensed muscles he pressed his arms against his thighs as he let the full weight of his body fall on the drill. With grim force he turned, bent and moved, his teeth clenched. The tension in his shoulder blades and back muscles went down through his thighs and calves until it became a living thing, and the miner a living sculpture of movement and strength. The coal fell down in chunks, and I scraped them away. Not a word was spoken. He was a simple boy in all his strength and dignity. Dripping with perspiration he rested a moment, wiping his black face on his black arms. I rested with him. Silently he sat down beside me.

We rested for only a moment, then went back to work. There were quite a number of Moroccans in this section. Not all of them could reconcile themselves to nudity; some kept their shorts on. But those were few.

I was called away to the end of the shaker conveyor. Through a hole in the wall and down a small ladder I climbed into the corridor where the coal was loaded into dump-carts. They were one man short. Here, too, everything was done in the nude. A few boys were squatting on top of the dump-carts to repair a crossbeam; others jumped over them, and still others were holding the beam up over their heads. Naked men pushed away the carts. Never did I notice any sign of sexual liberties. Nudity was never mentioned, not even outside the mine. I'd never heard about the conditions in this section until I saw them. They were taken for granted. In Varel they worked like that in all the mines. Many of the men had worked naked all their lives.

Now I understood why the director hadn't wanted me in Varel and why I had been carefully kept away from Rochy until now.

The chief engineer inquired about my experiences.

"It's pretty hard work," I said.

"Yes, but the men are nice, aren't they?"

"Yes, they are." Yet they didn't look nice at first sight. No wonder, really, for their work was anything but nice!

"I noticed there are a lot of Africans among the workers."

"Yes, curious people. An incredible sense of duty. They work hard, and you can rely on them. They're religious even in their work. Just think: most of these people, I should say more than ninety per cent, don't eat or drink all day during their long fasts."

"In Rochy too?"

"Yes. They can't eat until the moon comes up. And they rigorously adhere to that, even in Rochy."

"How is it possible?"

"They manage. They put many Catholics to shame."

Speak of the devil and he is sure to appear. There was a knock at the door. An African came in, a poor man, small as a schoolboy. He came to ask for work. The engineer was friendly but stern.

"You ran away without telling anybody. Now we can't take you back."

The man was crushed. He could hardly speak French.

"Really, it's impossible. Besides, we're not taking on any more men right now."

"But I was told to come to you . . . !"

The engineer made a gesture of helplessness.

"I haven't got any money left, sir," the African said in a hardly audible whisper. "I'd like to work . . . ."

"I'm sorry, but it's your own fault."

"What am I to do?"

"Look for work somewhere else."

"But they ask me where I worked before and why I left, and I haven't any papers."

"Come come, you can try again. Where are you living now?"

He mentioned a place where many Africans lived, and went away.

"You don't have to feel too sorry for him," the engineer said. "As long as this man doesn't have work he can live with his fellow countrymen. They won't let him starve; they always help each other."

The next day the foreman in Rochy took me to another section. The picture there was about the same. There was a Negro worker there, but you could tell it only by his kinky hair and thick lips, for everyone else was as black as he was. Only in the main corridor could I recognize the white race by its dirty gray color. A naked boy was lying down, guarding a side track, while other naked men, carrying a beam, stepped over him. A world apart that took things for granted with an ease unknown to the outside world.

22

I DIDN'T stay long in Rochy. I wanted to see the North of France, too, and didn't have too much time left. Besides, in Plouvy I found it very hard to keep up contact with the miners during their free time. Everyone went his own way. Many of them lived in neighboring villages or in town. There were no barracks where workers lived together, and I lived by myself in one of the mine buildings. Plouvy was an independent village, but it was within easy reach of the town. There wasn't the monotony of Filondange or St. Germain, where the workers were thrown back on themselves. Therefore there was a much less closely knit community life.

I was told about French social legislation, which is really excellent. Since the nationalization of the coal mines much had been done to modernize them. But there was a lot to be done yet.

The engineer asked how my experiences in the iron mines compared with what I had seen in Plouvy. I repeated my statements about the mental depression that takes hold of the workers, which was the same in Plouvy. Here, too — to a greater extent even because of the primitive conditions—the people felt they were "only" workers. But Plouvy had the advantage that the men could split up and find diversion in town. If Plouvy were an isolated village, the situation might become unbearable.

"Up to now," I said, "my experience has been that the workers become more human and better satisfied according to the degree of mechanization of their section. Of course, the mechanization shouldn't create other inhuman conditions, which give the worker the feeling that he's being sacrificed to machines and production."

The engineer was glad to hear me say this. They were hesitant about mechanizing because they feared it might cause discontent among the miners. The miners would be afraid of unemployment; unemployment in a country where industry cannot survive without employing foreign labor.

Why not consult the workers on the matter? I asked. Perhaps mechanization could be done with mutual consent. The engineer threw up his hands and said: "Save us from that! We tried that at the beginning of nationalization. We let the workers take part in the management of the mine. But they know nothing about it. They always talked about trivial things, a toilet here, a faucet there. No, we gave up that idea."

"Wouldn't it be possible to educate people at the mining school toward participation in management? It seems to me that would make the life of the worker more human, more dignified."

"But what does participation in management mean since the nationalization? Not much more than an empty formula. Just like sharing profits. Now the profits are meted out every so often in the form of a bonus. It's no longer a question of the profits of a concern, but of a whole group. What's left is not very much."

"You're not in favor of nationalization?"

"It has its advantages and disadvantages."

I also visited the mining school. Apart from their trade, the boys learned a little French there — like an extended primary education. In a small old mine, which was entrusted to them, they practised putting up shoring according to different systems. And every day they had exercises. Their health — their weight, the condition of their lungs, etc. — was checked regularly. The gym teacher showed off his program with pride and invited me to watch the health check-up. I noticed in many a certain shyness about undressing in the presence of a stranger — so there was no question of "crude" customs which passed from father to son. Probably the men from Rochy behaved like everyone else at home, and their sons were like all other boys who had no inhibitions about being naked in the shower room but did have them in the check-up room.

In Plouvy I saw my first Soviet movie, *Three Encounters*. The color technique was quite different from what we're used to in the West. The colors were warm and deep, and there was much reddish brown. The movie was about three soldiers who return to their native village and are anxious to accomplish something. The development of the theme was naive, but the moral standards depicted were lofty. The movie showed a world of honor and integrity and comradeship, where everyone could get ahead. The audience was fascinated. They probably believed not only in the possibility of all this, but in the reality of it. Besides, the Russian landscapes were of such beauty that the audience might really imagine that paradise wasn't lost after all. After a movie like that they could again believe that life was worth living. It was only a pity that this world was so far away.

A short about the conditioned reflexes of Pavlov's dogs was comprehensive, and it had more magnificent nature shots. When Stalin, the great fighter for this new world order, appeared on the screen there was spontaneous applause, and someone handed out propaganda leaflets. After the movie someone spoke on the subject of "being proud of 'our' ideal." Yes, all this appealed to the people. One has to be very critical indeed to keep clearly in mind that a movie can select what it wants. Apparently there were not many Communists in Plouvy, for the house was fairly empty. I knew that many hadn't come just because a Soviet movie was to be shown.

I went to see the parish priest, too. I had seen no sign of spiritual care for the workers. The pastor was out, but I was received by the curate in a waiting room. The parish house was very stylish. Yes, the curate said, it was a pity so few in the parish were practising. But there wasn't much one could do about it, that's just the way things were. He seemed resigned to being powerless.

There was no strong anti-clericalism in Plouvy, nor any strong anti-religious feeling. The Church and the clergy were taken for granted.

Before my departure for the North I put the finishing touches on my report to the Cardinal. It wasn't really much of a report: a great deal of it would have to be proved more conclusively.

I will give here only a brief résumé:

The common man lacks those intellectual powers which can be corrupted by arguments designed to convince him that God does not exist. Generally the expression "I do not believe" means more or less "I do not practise," completed eventually by "I do not know much about the Church and about Christ." Usually there is no doubt of the existence of God. All the same, the ignorance of religion among the workers can turn into agnosticism and skepticism, even with regard to the existence of God. This is not a strongly intellectual agnosticism or skepticism. What it amounts to is more or less this: life, the immediate reality about them, has a stronger impact on their minds than does the reality of God — in fact, than any other reality which does not lie on the surface of experience. In this superficial agnosticism there is still an underlying faith in God, in Christ, and even in the Church. At least they are still willing to be taught how God manifests Himself in Creation. But too often there is no one to explain it. Even though they don't practise, they retain a belief in the mediating function of the Church, and at the same time belief in eternal life.

I have talked with so many men who at first did not want to know anything about the Church. But even in them I found at bottom a touching religious sense. The Church in her actual structure does not make much impression on them. She knows everything of old, she is the vessel of a tradition — "ceremonial" and moral — the sense of which escapes them. They do not understand how carrying out the duties imposed by the Church can give meaning to life. Religion, in their view, should penetrate life, but not in a sense that is negative, prohibitive, or emasculating.

They accuse those who do practise of hypocrisy because they identify practising with the belief that one can save oneself by complying with formalities—and also, most of the time, because the churchgoers are capitalists, or the well-to-do.

According to the workers, the clergy that encourages such people and such formalism serves no purpose. This clergy maintains a religion unrelated to life and, since it renders no real service to men, it is a community of parasites on the body of society.

Personally I am convinced that beneath the indifferentism, beneath the irreligious and anti-religious attitudes, there is a desire to know whether Catholicism can yet offer anything vital. I do not see in this negative feeling towards the concrete practices of the Church that absence of the religious spirit, or of faith, which is asserted by many publications describing the dechristianization and paganization of the French working world. And there is more. I do not consider the indifferentism, and the manifestations of anti-religious feeling, merely as a negative factor; to me, on the contrary, they seem to be symptoms of a need—often explicit but still more often latent—for a return to the fundamental values of Catholicism.

They are looking for the meaning of life, and they do not see how the Church with its practices can give it. Indifferentism and anti-religious sentiment are moreover a warning that there is something about the practice of religion within the usual parish structure that is not adapted to our times. It may be that these people have a vocation to purify the Church, not in her essence but in her external manifestations. Instead of painting the picture in gloomy tones (undeniable though the ground for such an attitude may be), as the literature on the religious situation in France usually does, I prefer to emphasize the positive religious values hidden under this indifferentism. Very often, even continually, I have the sense that God is making use of these people to infuse new vitality into Catholicism: *Vox populi vox Dei* (not interpreted in the laicist sense) could almost mean here that we are being warned through the voice of the people to strip away the inessential and rediscover in our lives the true essence of Catholicism.

To sum up all my impressions, I must say that I have found in the working world the need for a sincere religious spirit that would give an ultimate meaning to life — to the whole of life as well as its details.

I would be very pessimistic if I confined myself to the immediate appearance of the working world. They do not speak of God, they do not fulfill the duties of a Catholic; apparently they do not pray; they accuse practising Catholics, the clergy, the Pope, of many failings—and often in an extremely vulgar tone; they blaspheme. The young people are brash and often vulgar in their talk and actions, and seem shameless. All considered, one could easily believe oneself to be in the midst of paganism. And yet . . . they truly think of God as *le bon Dieu*. One can sense their hope for eternal life after so much suffering. They suffer from their own vulgarity; and this already implies a need, even a desire, to live according to the true meaning of life. They are sincere—that is, they yield to whatever argument succeeds in convincing them. They do not run away from ideas which conflict with their own.

I could say, especially with regard to the miners, that the arduous labor absorbs them and brutalizes them. They become hard, like the material they work with. Often they seem to have become unapproachable, but in reality they have remained children, happy over little things and sensitive to the slightest attentions.

In the working world is found an elemental human simplicity. The workers hate formalism, the façade of hypocrisy. In this world one is faced with the essence of human nature, avenging itself against the various distortions which have been imposed on it during the course of our cultural, and even of our religious, development, and which have become empty forms, no longer conveying the meaning they once contained.

The working world suffers more or less from the formalistic culture and from the façades of a religiosity in which it does not participate. Their "betters" who surround them—the capitalists —who are the representatives of this culture and this religiosity, have thought of the workers as a "force" which is "used" (or is impoverished) for "gain." The worker is not valued primarily as a man, but rather for his contribution to this gain.

The social organizations have improved the conditions of the worker's life, but not the structure of the work itself. To be more precise, they who suffer injustice continue to be used like an inanimate force. All this has created an inferiority complex in the working world. This sense of inferiority shows itself in the great responsiveness of the workers to every attention and sign of regard shown them. The same sense of inferiority seeks compensation in boasting among fellow workers and in explosions of revolt; or it dulls itself with alcohol or in the satisfaction of elemental passions.

Communism has stirred up this natural resistance, though at the cost of a certain disorientation of its own doctrine. Communism is not very strong now in the areas that I know. The workers are even disillusioned with Communism, and tired of it. But the resistance remains beneath the surface. It is a resistance first of all not against capital but against injustice; and, since they consider capitalism bound up with traditional culture and religion, it is also a resistance (always ready to break out into a revolution) against the façade of culture and religion.

However, this does not mean that culture, and still less religion, has no longer any value for the working world. What they want is justice, simplicity, sincerity; a true regard for man; and a vital religion.

This latent resistance will in my opinion have a purifying action on culture and religious life. I believe it is important to recognize all this under the surface appearances of the working world, depressing as these are. I also believe that we can already see the influence of the working world on actual society and in a certain re-evaluation of religious values.

The priest of St. Thomas's church had more than once expressed his curiosity as to what I would write to the Cardinal. I didn't feel like showing him the letter, but when he invited me to dinner along with his two worker-priests I knew I couldn't escape it. Before dinner was over one of the worker-priests got up: he had not time to stay to the end. At that point the parish priest asked me directly: "Tell us briefly the contents of your report. You didn't say anything bad about us, did you?"

"No."

Why shouldn't I show them the letter after all? I handed it to the priest.

"You may not agree with many of my statements."

"We'll see." He began reading aloud at an incredibly fast rate, while the two worker-priests looked over his shoulder. The one who had to leave had already put his beret on. They read so fast that I wondered whether they could get the meaning of it. The priest underlined sentences by nodding his head.

"Good," said the man who was on the point of going. He shook hands with me warmly and went out.

"Good," the others said too. They gave me back the letter. There was no further comment.

We went on talking for a while until I stood up. I couldn't

stay too late, as I was leaving the next morning for Paris. I had just told them about the Soviet movie I had seen. The priest was more or less surprised that I could find so many good qualities in it. He was surprised, too, that such films were allowed in France. He hadn't seen it himself. But the worker-priest who was still there agreed with me. When I left, he left too. He said he'd take me to the streetcar. Actually, he wanted to talk a few things over with me. We were both wearing jackets and berets, like so many others, but our conversation was less casual than that of most. We walked past several stops and let many streetcars go by. I asked him whether he really agreed with what I had written to the Cardinal.

He was very frank and said: "Yes, but you're only on the threshold of the truth. If you'd follow these people into their lives, you'd see that there is nothing left there of the religious sentiments they utter at unguarded moments."

"But what is the truth, the sentiments of their lives?"

He didn't reply. We walked on in silence under the street lights. Did he, too, doubt that a foreigner could get an accurate picture of the situation in so short a time?

Yet knowing people doesn't depend only on a length of time, nor do the detailed, standardized questions of a formal interview necessarily reveal the true nature of a man. One has to have the gift of understanding people. One can get to know a man's inmost nature in an unguarded moment, by a single phrase, a cry. And when one has discovered him in this way one may, as the great Spanish author Unamuno says, know him better than he knows himself. I believe there's a great deal of truth in this. The difference between man's inner being and his exterior mask is undefinable, but it is there all the same. The symptoms and symbolism of everyday behavior must be understood and interpreted correctly.

By the same token objective, theologically defined and strictly prescribed religious criteria are not enough to judge whether a person is religious or not. One must also find out whether objective values and truths are still present in a man's personal sense of religion. Had my experiences really carried me only to the threshold of the truth? Would I get a different picture if I were to stay for years in the same milieu? Of course man grows with time, but he is not moulded entirely from the outside. What he is, is a combination of circumstances and his inner self. And this "self" can be revealed in a stray moment.

It takes a certain amount of time to know the daily circumstances people have to cope with. But can't the main lines be discerned in a month? Imagine someone participating in monastery life for a month to get an idea of it. If he kept his eyes and ears open, he could get a pretty accurate picture of it in that time. One could hardly reproach him for not having a true picture because he didn't participate in a general chapter. A general chapter doesn't change monastery life, anyway. If the same man goes to another monastery for another month, and then to another for the same length of time, his experience is more or less complete. Except for some daily nuances he will not discover anything essentially new. He has found the standard which is characteristic of all monastery life. From these experiences he can even understand the difficulties of monastic life.

My friend was apparently not aware of the purport of what he had said. He thought I had done important work and was anxious to know the final outcome of it.

Or was his praise nothing but courtesy?

I kept in touch with the people at Plouvy, with Jean, with my host and even with the director-general. And there even came an unexpected card from the good parish priest at St. Thomas's. It seemed that they did not hold my work to be as unfruitful as I feared. They urged with one voice that I come and see them again. Meanwhile, through my contacts with friends I was living like a sort of United Nations collected into one.

So many lives live in my life, and vice versa, after having touched one another in such a personal manner. So many times at the strangest moments there pass through my memory and my feelings men who for me are now only a name and a place.

And there are still so many others with whom I am no longer in touch. Why name them here? I am bound to them by life, in its transience and in its human beauty, in its distractions and in its suffering. I cannot, like Saint Paul, boast of being shipwrecked or beaten; perhaps I cannot boast of anything. He who praises himself is not worth very much.

23

I WANTED to visit Father Egidius and a few others in Paris. I also wanted to become acquainted, if possible, with the Mission de Paris, Catholic Action, the JOC and the Confederation Française des Travailleurs Chretiens (CFTC) to have my experiences and impressions criticized by the chief authorities of French Catholicism.

Close to my hotel, at the Boulevard Voltaire, stood a church. I said Mass there the next morning. Afterward a venerable, gray-haired priest invited me to breakfast at the rectory. He asked about my work, and the conversation became quite confidential. Yes, he did respect the efforts of the worker-priests. Only he thought that sometimes they painted the religious situation in the workers' world too black. He had never met any of these pagans he had heard so much about. He didn't want to deny their existence, but as for claiming that they represented the largest part of the workers' world — no, that was pure imagination. He hadn't had such tragic experiences, even with people who hadn't been baptized. Once in a while a worker would even come to him with the complaint that he was a Catholic but that no one had ever baptized him, and it was about time. And they came of their own free will, not because of a marriage or some such occasion. People weren't so bad, but there was widespread ignorance.

I was surprised at what he said. Partly he confirmed my own impressions. But I wondered how he could judge what really went on if he dealt only with people who sought contact with the clergy. Did he simply suppose that the ones who stayed away were no different? Or did he judge from wisdom and a mature knowledge of humanity? Or was it chauvinism: did he refuse to believe that France was no longer a Catholic country, as so many maintained nowadays? Or were his opinions prompted by a need for reassurance, in view of the fact that in his parish of more than fifty thousand souls only an extremely low percentage was practising? I thought his attitude must surely irritate the worker-priests. Yet I could only endorse his views, and the activities of the worker-priests as well. The latter might paint the picture somewhat too black, but their missionary work certainly filled a real need.

It was afternoon by the time I boarded a train for Arras at the Gare du Nord. I wanted to visit Abbé L., whom I'd met in Arbresle, and inform him of my plans to work in the North. If he heard about it later without my having told him, he might take it as a slight, and I wanted to avoid that. I arrived full of a feeling of loneliness. How long would I be able to keep up this running around? Out of pure self-indulgence I ate expensively that evening — Chateaubriand. Yes, I thought, I surely was a man with expensive tastes if I let myself go.

The Abbé L. was out of town.

I went on to Lille, where I wanted to look up Abbé Dupont whom I had also met in Arbresle. I noticed that restaurants and hotels were much more expensive in the North. In a dilapidated Flemish hotel where, in spite of the name, they spoke only

French, I slept in a room whose only window opened onto the stairs. It was always dark inside. But the landlady busily lit a fire for me in the pot-bellied stove. I saw a banal movie and went to sleep exhausted as a tramp. I couldn't keep this up. I decided then and there to stay only a short time in the North.

Abbé Dupont received me as a good friend. He had much appreciation for what I told him. He himself had just finished a statistical study of the practice of religion in the diocese of Lille, and he gave me his material. I told him about my visit to the Cardinal in Lyons and the report I had written for him. Couldn't he have a look at it?

"Yes, but I'd rather you wouldn't talk about it, or at any rate not refer to it publicly. After all, it isn't an open letter."

He read it while I went through the papers he had given me. Abbé Fourier came in. There were several priests living in the house. It was a kind of social-welfare center. Abbé Fourier was a man of great warmth with many interests.

"You should let him read the letter, too," said Abbé Dupont. "It'll please him."

I nodded, and he passed the letter on.

"He sees in a few months what takes us years to see! It certainly is an advantage to be a foreigner and to be able to compare different countries. We have difficulty getting rid of certain views that happen to be fashionable among us. Your kind of research has never really been done here before. We judge by given data and by suggestions. It would be worthwhile to discuss your letter in various circles, especially among the higher clergy."

"Can we make a copy of it?" asked Abbé Fourier.

"I wouldn't like the letter to be circulated in this form."

"No, no, just for our own use. We won't take advantage of it."

"If you really won't, go ahead. I hope I'm orthodox with my suggestions that preaching and other forms of the apostolate should begin with an analysis of human existence."

Abbé Dupont smiled. "Don't worry. We Frenchmen all have a tendency to be a little heterodox. We like to take risks."

That evening I traveled on to Calence. I had the visiting card of Abbé Dupont to introduce myself to a priest who would be able to tell me a lot about the workers in the North. After some searching in dark little streets I found him. He lived very simply and received me cordially.

I was getting tired of having to tell again and again what my plans were and what I had done so far.

This time I was dealing with a serious man who, unintentionally and out of genuine love for the workers, almost dealt me a death-blow. I hadn't yet mentioned the work I had done. I began by explaining that the mine director in Calence would probably allow me to work in one of his mines; that I wanted to do this in order to learn the spiritual problems of the workers. Then I asked him for information about finding a place to live among the workers in this area.

"I could put you up with a worker's family," he replied. "But this kind of situation is very delicate. Some time ago another young priest wanted to serve an apprenticeship in the mines. I found him a place to live. But he took advantage of his position and behaved deplorably. You understand that this way things are destroyed that have been built up with great difficulty. And another thing: believe me, you have to be a real worker if you want to understand the workers. The Lord save us from those spiritual adventurers who think they can understand and judge everything in a few months. Also, the misery of others is not something to experiment on. It's insulting to use it to satisfy a desire for sensation."

I didn't say any more about my studies and didn't mention that I had worked in the mines already. I hadn't the courage to say anything in my own defense. If he had put me out of the house, I might have lain down on the street to sleep.

He didn't speak arrogantly, but out of a genuine respect for reality. This made me helpless. And he remained friendly to the end.

"When you have seen the director and you know where you're going to work, I'm willing to try and find you a place to live."

"Thank you. I think I shall find my way. I only have to find a place for tonight."

"If you can make do with a sleeping bag, you can stay here. There's still some stuff here from Catholic Action members, and we have a small dormitory. There's only one boy staying here tonight. Tomorrow I'm saying Mass at the sisters' nearby. You can come with me if you like."

The dormitory was ice-cold. The Catholic Action boy was bundled up and fast asleep when I came in. The Abbé slept with as little comfort as we had, in a private room.

It was ice-cold, too, in the chapel where we said Mass the next morning, and also in the room where we had breakfast. But I was told I would always be welcome at these sisters' chapel whenever I wanted to say Mass in Calence.

In the administration building I had to fill out a form stating the reason for my visit. I wrote that I had been sent by the mine director in Varel, and the form was taken to the director's office. I had been waiting for over an hour when finally a fatherly, somewhat mannered engineer came for me. The director had asked him to take care of me. He listened to my story and thought he might be able to comply with my request to be an apprentice without pay. But he did have to report back to the director, who didn't know I was a priest. There had been no phone call from Varel as yet, but he didn't think there would be any objection. The director himself came in for a moment. He didn't have any objections, but he gave me to understand coldly and matter-of-factly that I would have to do actual work without getting paid for it, for he couldn't release anybody for any length of time to show me the mine. I said I hadn't counted on being treated as a visitor. On that condition, he agreed. He left me to the engineer, who would arrange everything.

The question of where to put me posed a problem.

"Aren't there any barracks or workers' camps?" I asked.

"Workers' camps, yes . . ." he looked at me doubtfully. "All right, I'll write you out a ticket for camp Plaignac. You can work in the mine there."

He called the chief of personnel and took me in his car to the camp, about twelve miles from Calence. On the way he pointed out his office to me, so I would be able to find him in case of difficulties. I asked him not to take me all the way to the camp; he could put me off somewhere nearby and I would find my way.

24

PLAIGNAC turned out to be a former concentration camp. It was a small village of barracks in the open fields, fenced off by poles and wire. Most of the barracks were divided into three sections and inhabited by about twelve workers. In the center of the camp was a section for administration and supply storage and another one that served as kitchen and dining room.

"Ah, a new man," said the camp boss. I was registered and got a ration card, two tin plates and a mug. I would have to sleep in barracks no. 8, and I was given some bedding: a mattress, a sheet sewn together like a bag, and some blankets. I could take all this to the barracks as soon as the workers returned from the mine, for now everything was locked. The boss showed me a barracks where the inhabitants were home and where I could stay until I could get into my own quarters.

I knocked and went in. *"Bonjour."*

"Bonjour." In each corner of the room stood a bed, and on three of them lay my new co-workers. One of them rubbed his eyes sleepily and looked at me with curiosity; another was lying

with his knees pulled up, reading a magazine, from behind which he looked me over in surprise. A woman was sitting next to him on a stool. A third young man sat up as I came in.

"Is it all right if I come in?" I asked, not knowing what else to say.

"Sure."

"Can I bother you for an hour? I've nowhere to go till the others come back."

"Oh, a new man." The sleepy boy sat up, too. "Sit down."

A little pot-bellied stove had made the room drowsily warm. Some shirts were drying on a wire. The floor was dirty, the walls looked unpainted. I asked their names and told them mine.

"Are you a regular worker or an apprentice?" they wanted to know.

"I guess it depends on what kind of work they'll give me tomorrow."

Why? Had I worked in the mines before? Yes, I had. They wanted to know where and I told them.

"Well, you're out of luck," they said. "It's an old mine here. In Pas de Calais it's much more modern."

"Why don't you go there yourselves?"

"It's difficult to get in. It's getting more and more mechanized, and more and more men are laid off."

"They do what they like with you these days," said the young man who was reading the magazine. "They sent me here from Calais with the guarantee that I'd get a house. This is my wife. Well, you can see for yourself. I've been here for a few months now. I can go to the housing bureau as often as I like, and every time they tell me it'll be taken care of; it'll always be taken care of. You can drop dead for all they care. A fine beginning for a marriage. Our furniture and our radio are still packed."

"That gypsy over there," said the youth next to me, pointing to the third man, "is from Marseilles. You better not quarrel with him; he's a fighter."

The gypsy from Marseilles hitched up his pants and came toward us. He also had something to say.

"It's a scandal. And that in France, the most modern country in Europe, and a leader in culture! Have you seen the camp yet? You should see where the Africans live. They've got holes in the floor."

"You don't have to go to the Africans for that. Can you tell me which barracks here has a decent floor?" added one of the others.

"It seems I have bad luck," I remarked.

"Bad luck? No matter what camp in the North, it's the same everywhere. Have you seen our toilets?"

"Not yet."

"They're just dandy! A paradise for flies in the summer." He gestured to indicate how wonderful it all was.

We talked on in this vein until I got up to see if I could get into my own barracks and get a meal.

"You know where we live now," the men said.

"Yes; see you later."

The barracks where I was to live stood at the camp entrance. Two thirds of it was inhabited by a married worker, to whom it had been assigned as a temporary home. He had carefully fenced off small strips of garden in front and in back of the barracks and apparently didn't want to have anything to do with anybody. This meant that the men in the remaining part couldn't use the sink or the toilet, which were meant for the whole barracks. Whether this was just or unjust, the fact remained that it had been turned into private property. The men with whom I was to share the fourth room had to manage as best they could. Water was obtained a few barracks away in a wash basin. During the day it served as drinking water, early in the morning for washing. We had to take out water with a mug for dishwashing and shaving.

When I arrived one of my new neighbors was chopping wood in front of the door. They had just returned, and it was cold inside. A second man was sweeping the room. Both of them were Italians, or rather Sicilians. They hadn't known about my coming, and were rather surprised that I had been put with them. After all, the administration knew that the brother of one of them was to return shortly. He was now on a long leave to be married in Sicily, but he had always slept here. Well, anyway, I'd better go and bring my things and get settled. No, I'd better eat first; otherwise it would be too late for that.

Against the wall stood a small table with pots, pans, bottles and other things. There were two benches for two people each. We had to make do with that.

Armed with my ration card, two plates, fork, knife and spoon I set out for the dining room.

"Just take your plates," they told me. "Nobody eats over there. They all eat in their barracks."

As I waited my turn in the dining room, I saw why no one wanted to eat there. The room was unpainted, unheated and generally cheerless. The barracks were unpainted, too, but at least it was warm inside and you were among friends.

I maneuvered my way back to the barracks with a plate of soup in one hand and a plate of potatoes, vegetables and meat in the other; a distance of several hundred yards. This was to be repeated twice a day, in rain, cold and wind, shuffling in the dark at night and calling "Look out!" whenever you met somebody.

I didn't have any bread yet; each man had to go out and buy that. But my friends shared theirs with me. I'd go shopping in the course of the afternoon. I had to hang everything edible on a nail against the wall, they warned me; otherwise the mice would get it.

After dinner I went to the mine to check in. The engineer had told them I was coming. I had my own overalls and working shoes from the iron mines, so all I needed was a helmet and a lamp and a number for the shower room. There was no room left in the big shower room. I was put with about ten men who used a small side-building. They told me where and to whom to report the next morning at six, and then I was free to leave.

My roommates worked in another mine a short distance away. They said they'd hide the door key in the mud under the garbage pail, so I could get in if I was back earlier than they.

I soon noticed that the men of the different barracks didn't mix much. Away from work they remained strangers; many were of different nationalities.

In the evening after dinner I inquired what was going on in the camp and in the neighborhood. Yawning with boredom one of my roommates answered: "Nothing, absolutely nothing . . . It's always the same thing. The pit, the pit, the pit, today, tomorrow and always." He stretched. "And when you get back, dead beat, well, then you can eat and go to sleep. The pit, eating and sleeping, that's all. What goes on here? Nothing, absolutely nothing. Prison life. You can go to the village, of course. But what do you get there? Nothing. That's our life. Always the same thing. It's no life. And when we come to the good Lord, what can we tell Him? Nothing. That we did nothing but work underground, sleep and eat. That's all." He turned his head away from us on his dirty pillow.

We went to sleep. That is to say, we turned off the light and I dozed off. But it wasn't long before I was wide awake again. A mouse ran full-speed over my face. I saw others running over my blankets. I sat up in the dark. This was too much. At my sudden movement they stopped squeaking. After a while I lay down again, and the fun started again. My comrades seemed used to it. Well, if nothing could be done about it, I would just have to learn to sleep with mice running over me. And I slept.

The next morning we carefully shared the water in the wash basin, swallowed some coffee, ate a few mouthfuls of bread, and left. The key was put under the garbage pail. Silently we walked together in the dark until I had to turn off. In the shower room I met some of my fellow workers, changed into working clothes, and went with them to the mine. There were a few hundred of us waiting our turns to go down. Our group consisted of ten Africans and ten Frenchmen. The Africans were very particular:

they pointed out to me that my coffee jar was too big. You couldn't take such large glass objects down with you! But their remarks were friendly.

I worked with two young, silent Frenchmen. Scooping coal into dump-carts and carrying sections of track had become somewhat of a specialty of mine. After each blast they worked for a while with dust masks on. No longer than necessary, for they choked you, they said. I didn't have a mask and had to get out of the way during the dust periods; otherwise, they warned, it would be suicide.

Why St. Barbara should be the patron saint of the mines I don't know, but she is, and the miners esteem her highly. In one of the corridors was a niche made specially for a statue of her; a hideous statue, but that didn't matter. I asked my friends for an explanation, and they threw up their hands in surprise. What kind of a country was Holland? Didn't they have St. Barbara there? Her name day was early in December, the biggest festival of the year. They got the day off and celebrated. It was their day.

I was there when it took place, and the day was celebrated very "liturgically," for it started with a "first vespers": they had smuggled some gin into the pits, and after lunch nobody did any work. The foremen knew their boys and let them have their fun.

There was no evidence of a religious celebration. The boys were bored, as always. Only their boredom was a little festive because it was St. Barbara's day. My roommates came back from the mine in high spirits, and while we were chopping wood and tidying up the room, the woman from the barracks next door came in. She was a tough one and didn't stand for any nonsense. She sat on the edge of one of the beds and listened to the tall stories that were being told, heavily studded with oaths. But she stood her ground. "Don't make fun of God, will you!" she snapped at one of the men.

Make fun of God? What was she thinking? My goodness, the man wasn't making fun of God at all.

"Yes, but those expressions — you'd better be careful. If God ever got serious, you'd get it."

My friend withdrew into his shell. What if it were true!

"Don't think I have no faith," he defended himself. "I always believe in everything, except in priests. I just say things without thinking. But I do believe in the good Lord, always. And in Her!" With his roguish, childlike face he looked at a small picture of Mary over his bed.

"I may curse all day, but that's because I don't think about it. At night under the blankets I always say a prayer."

The woman didn't stoop to reply. "Mary will put in a good word for me," he went on, cheerful as a little boy. The woman stood up and left.

He started dancing through the room, opened his locker and triumphantly produced a brassière, which he kissed out of sheer exuberance.

"A souvenir!"

"A souvenir?"

"What a pity she isn't here any more. A Spanish girl from last year."

He made gestures to show what a fine figure the girl had had. To the great amusement of his friends, he put on the brassière himself and draped a blanket around him.

That evening I visited the barracks where I had spent my first hour in the camp. For some time there had been a newcomer there, a Yugoslav, obviously not a miner but an educated man of about thirty: dark, quiet, civilized and friendly. His roommates began telling me about him. Some guy he was, they said. He spoke Greek and Russian, Italian, Spanish, English, German and French. The Yugoslav listened in silence. Nobody seemed to wonder what he was doing in the mine.

One afternoon I found him alone. We walked around for a while.

"How do you like it here," I asked him, "and what made you come here in the first place? You don't look like a miner."

He smiled meaningly and replied: "You don't, either!" I smiled, too. "What did you study before you came here?" I asked.

"At a technical school."

"Do you need so many languages for that?"

"No, I picked them up. I've traveled around."

I didn't inquire any further. He didn't ask what I was doing in the mine, either. But we got along very well. He only wanted to know: "Are the girls around here anything special?"

"What do you expect? It's the same here as everywhere."

He laughed.

On St. Barbara's night we all had a talk in his barracks. He had good tobacco, and he shared it with us. The gypsy from Marseilles had had a fight with a Pole in the next room. The gypsy had lost and now sat listening in silence. Suddenly he got up without a word and left, probably to get drunk in the village or to go to a dance or to find a girl with whom he could forget his sorrow.

The Pole came in. Did anyone want to go to the movies? Only one of us felt like it.

"Won't you come along?" asked the youth on whose bed I was sitting.

"All right," I agreed.

The three of us left, the Pole in the middle. He wasn't quite drunk yet, but he was not far from it. It was after midnight when we came home.

"My pal's got his girl with him again," said the Pole as he walked to his own barracks. "It's the same thing every night. So long."

The next day was a Sunday, and I went to Calence to say Mass at the sisters'. I asked Mother Superior for a scapular, for I had lost mine. She came back with a handful of them.

"Oh, I only need one!"

"The others are for the workers."

I smiled. Well meant, but I hadn't got to the point of handing out scapulars.

I didn't return to the camp till evening. They wouldn't have understood why I wouldn't sit in bars all day or go to a dance.

My roommates were cleaning up the room.

"What's going on here?" I asked.

They laughed. One of them winked and put a finger to his lips.

"Tonight." He pantomimed hugging and kissing a girl.

"Oh, is that it?"

"Yes, she's coming here. Keep it to yourself, will you?"

Officially women were not allowed in the camp, but actually the restriction might as well not have existed.

"What time is she coming?"

"About ten o'clock."

"As long as you know I have to get up at five. I'm going to bed."

"Where were you today?"

"In Calence."

"You go a long way for love."

"Oh, yes."

The evening turned out to be a disappointment for him: the mademoiselle didn't show up.

The parish priest agreed with me that there was much more religious feeling among the workers than was generally supposed.

"Curious," he remarked. "They don't come to church. But I know about ten of them, for instance, that got together on their own initiative to read and study the Gospels. They're enthusiastic about it. Once in a while they come to me and ask me to explain things they don't understand. They're extremely happy with what they learn that way. They're Catholics in their own way. But I wouldn't dare point out any formal obligations to them. They wouldn't understand. It's as if I'd be destroying something in them, as if I'd be forcing them into a straitjacket. I believe they live spontaneously according to the Gospel, but the Gospels are concerned with real life and that's why they are acceptable to them."

"And if you should ask them to come to Mass every Sunday

and go to confession and receive Communion, they would probably feel that as a formalizing of their religion, wouldn't they?" I mused.

"Exactly. They'd be willing to confess their sins and also to receive our Lord, but in an intimate, spontaneous way. The liturgy, official church-going, that's not for them. Christ would suddenly assume a very different appearance for them."

"If only one could celebrate Mass and Communion with them in their own little groups," I said to him. "From such a nucleus a bigger Christian community could emerge, based on life itself.

"With some new forms, perhaps. Yet I believe many of the old forms might appeal to them again as meaningful and beautiful. We have so many standardized, traditional forms of worship which people have to observe if they want to be good Catholics. That's why we think there are so few good Catholics. In the ignorance of their religion people may do many things that are not in accordance with the spirit of Christianity, but it remains to be seen whether their pastors should educate them right away toward the less important traditional forms, which aren't so important after all, or begin with the Gospel and gradually build up the official community forms of worship with their people, saving as much of the old ritual as possible. After all, the sacramental contact with Christ can be accomplished in many ways. And the preaching of the eternal truths, too."

"Yes," he retorted, "but in this respect we're not free to do as we like. Our methods are prescribed and Rome doesn't deviate from the traditional forms."

"True," I admitted, "the Church wants to avoid chaos, of course, but it doesn't prevent us from finding new ways and means for spiritual care."

About an hour later I walked through the cold December streets, my hands in my pockets. I was still thinking of our conversation, and of the role of the clergy in modern society. A priest in a cassock is to many people a being from another world, something holy perhaps, but at the same time something quite different

from them. The distance is lessened when a priest goes about
dressed the same way they are. Suppose he gets permission to
move among the people the way he wants to, and gains confidence and a spiritual authority in various circles. Suppose he
succeeds in making people realize the beauty of the Gospel, so
that love for Christ becomes the guiding factor in their lives. If
he then wanted to bring back the offering of Christ in their midst,
he couldn't do it so easily. He couldn't end an ordinary meeting
with the celebration of Mass. Yet it could be a tremendous reality
for people if among them the bread could be broken which is the
body of Christ.

Priests might be able to conquer the world for Christ, as the
apostles did, but within the liturgy many forms of secondary
importance no longer correspond to the spirit of the times, as they
did at the beginning of our era. The Gospel appeals to people;
many liturgical and religious obligations don't. The Gospel has
been reduced to a vague awareness in their minds, but at least
it's still there, and it could again be made into a compelling truth.
It seems, however, that many don't consider this Catholicism, or
even a desire for Catholicism. To countless people being a Catholic means living according to liturgical and religious prescrip-
tions. Many accept only the outward formalities of the Church
instead of its essence. Among the people Christ lives in exile—a
Christ without ritual. But the Church is wherever Christ is among
the people in His sacraments and in His truth.

My work in camp Plaignac had come to an end. I said good-bye
to my friends, spent one afternoon visiting the nearby mining
school where an accelerated course was given for fifty newly
arrived young Africans—(there were about 300,000 of them in
France at that moment)—and finally went to say good-bye to the
engineer. Since he was the one in charge of housing and of the
camps, it was his official duty to ask me whether I'd had everything I needed.

"What do you want me to say?" I replied. "I survived, as you

see, and my only wish was to share the life of the workers. You
made it possible, and I'm grateful to you for it. I've come to tell
you this once again."

He smiled.

"Did you notice anything that wasn't all that it should be, anything we could or should change?"

He asked me this as though he knew I was intelligent and
reasonable enough to see that everything possible was being done
for the workers.

"May I tell you briefly what my impressions are?" I asked.

"Of course, of course."

"In the first place, the camp is beautifully situated, out in the
open fields and very quiet."

He gave a nod of agreement.

"But I must say, it's pretty deadly. Not only is there no comfort, but there isn't any opportunity for cultural recreation. The
boys are doomed to vegetation in their free time."

I saw that he didn't care to go into the subject. "Well," he said
casually, "they're only there for a short time. Naturally a camp
is not an ideal place. It's an emergency solution, so to speak. Our
aim is to make the men feel at home."

It's wonderful, of course, if you can quiet your conscience with
only an aim. And he was pleased that I appreciated his efforts.
As far as he was concerned, there wasn't any more to say, and
he went on to the next question:

"Was the food all right?"

"The food was all right, but there wasn't enough for people
who do heavy work."

He smiled. "Yes, we purposely keep it that way, you see; otherwise there's going to be cheating. They can buy additional food
if they want to."

"They have to, if they want to keep going. The worst is that
the camp is so dull. You may have plans to change all that in the
future, but meanwhile the men are bored to death in the camp
for years on end. In most of the barracks the floors are caving in,

the mice run over you at night . . . ." (He made a face as if to say: it isn't nice of you to say these things just before you leave) ". . . and then there are the married men who are desperate because they're put in a camp when they've been promised homes."

He interrupted: "That's only for a short time. They'll be taken care of."

The men themselves were given the run-around with that story, too. Of course, I said, each case couldn't be dealt with right away, but how were the men expected to feel when they saw that everything could be arranged if they had connections, but if they hadn't they simply had to take what they could get?

"I understand that it's very difficult at times," I conceded. "But couldn't something at least be done for them in a cultural way?"

"Did you know that the YMCA organizes regular concerts here for the workers?" he asked me. "Really very cultural events. But hardly anybody goes to listen."

I thought of Plouvy. There the workers were not ready for participation in management. Here they were not ready for cultural life. And that diagnosis was excuse enough to leave them to their fate.

"Wouldn't it be possible," I continued, "to train the young workers not just technically, but to give them some sort of education that would enable them to remain mentally alert, in spite of their heavy work? When it comes to things involving the good of the industry, every little detail is attended to. But where the men are concerned a stopgap is good enough. And when the stopgap proves insufficient the general feeling is: why should we bother? The wound will heal itself."

The engineer smiled amiably. Everything would remain as it was. Any change would have to come from higher up. One man alone couldn't even start anything.

25

I RETURNED to Paris via Lille. There I found only Abbé Dupont; Abbé Fourier wasn't in. But shortly after my arrival in Paris I received a short and cordial note from him, and some money:

Lille, 8-12-'51

Dear Father,

I'm sorry I was out when you called. I heard that you were very tired and I'm worried that you don't have any warm clothes for this time of year. Is there anything I can do for you? At least accept this small amount of money as a friend.

Enclosed is your report, which interested us greatly. I have taken the liberty of making two copies of it: one for Abbé Dupont and one for myself. We will use it very discreetly.

May Our Lord, through the intercession of the Blessed Virgin, enable you to pass on the Good Word to the souls of the workers.

Abbé F. Fourier.

So they had noticed that I was tired. It was written in black and white, like an unsolicited diagnosis, by a priest who had seen me for only a few hours. I knew I had to stop: I was exhausted, not so much physically as mentally. But how could I stop? I had worn myself out because I couldn't go through life neutrally, as an outsider. I was tortured by a sense of powerlessness. I had arrived at the limits of my own insignificance. I had to accept them or become desperate. God and life would go their own ways; they didn't depend on me; I should know better than that. In

God's Providence people were safe, safer than in the grip of my ideas. I hoped that God would preserve all those people who were in search of Him—people whom I loved, known and unknown—for Himself. I hoped He would change the harm I might do others into good. (And how many ways are there of doing harm? By uttering a thought, by suggesting doubts, by behaving in a way that could be misunderstood.) I hoped too that I might not be an obstacle to simple people in their search for God.

But weren't my fatigue and the simultaneous realization of my own impotence a sign of lack of confidence on my part, and surrender? I had come to an almost continual, unspoken repetition of *"Vide, Domine, et miserere."*

I had been given leave to go to Holland for a rest and to settle some personal affairs before returning to Rome. I wanted to celebrate Christmas in my native country, and I had two weeks left to discuss my experiences and impressions in Paris. Father Egidius was of the opinion that I would have a hard time finding work in Paris itself. But I had given up that idea, anyway.

What I discussed with him and some other professors, with the directors of Catholic Action and with others from the Mission de Paris and the Mission de France, came down more or less to this; and might, indeed, serve as a summary of the experiences and reflections described within this book.

On the basis of statistics a picture of the religious situation in France emerges that, on the facts alone, I cannot deny. The interpretation, however, is a different matter. The facts seem clearly to indicate that France has been largely dechristianized and that the workers' world has become thoroughly pagan.

The facts of the situation, that religious obligations are no longer carried out—or scarcely ever—and that the sacraments are no longer—or seldom—received, do indicate that there is something wrong with the Catholicism of the people. One can wonder with good reason whether people who don't recognize the value of these obligations can still be called Christians. After all, these symptoms obviously prove the lack of a living Catholic faith. Consequently the conclusion that France has become de-christianized is considered correct. Moreover, the moral lives of these people seem amply to confirm this assumption. Between them and true Christians lies a great chasm. And when one is no longer a true Christian, what is one? A sectarian? This would mean a lively interest in at least certain religious values. But a heterodox religious interest is certainly not characteristic of modern French society. On the contrary, what is evident is a lack of religious interest of any kind. People are indifferent. The interests they do have are completely earthly and materialistic. One might say, and many do, that Catholicism has been replaced by a materialistic and naturalistic outlook on life.

Numerous studies have been made to explain the causes of the present situation. They turn out to be of a sociological, psychological and ideological nature. And again the conclusion is drawn that the religious state of affairs in many milieus in France can no longer be called Christian.

Once this has been established, nothing remains but to reject as worthless the statistics to the contrary, which show that the great majority of the French population has been baptized; that the great majority of the children are still being baptized and are receiving their first Communion; that a high percentage of people are married in the Church and have Church burials. These things are seen as nothing but folk habits, as traditions which have nothing to do with faith, since it has already been concluded that faith no longer exists.

These objective conclusions are supposedly drawn from facts. However, one important thing is overlooked: namely that, as I have already pointed out, people don't reason or act like professional theologians and moralists. Statistics are purely objective by nature, and in this case the interpretation of them has often not gone beyond their face value. Even the so-called reality outside the statistics is often viewed from a too-theological point of view.

So that the reality, too, appears to confirm the interpretations of the statistics. There seems to be no way out. The situation, one is quite sure, is seen realistically.

But meanwhile too little effort has been made to ascertain whether these supposedly objective conclusions actually correspond to reality. It is not enough to reason theologically, or to draw conclusions regarding people's religious convictions on the basis of certain "formal" practices. It is necessary to observe people in their own surroundings, or share their lives, to find out what religious feelings they still have.

I have tried to do this. My impressions cannot be put down in terms of numbers. I stayed in different workers' groups only long enough to get a sufficient impression of them, until there was nothing new to see or hear. My interpretation of the statistics differs from the customary one. To me the value of these statistics is that they indicate to what extent the outlook on life is found which I have come to know. They remain indispensable for seeing the picture of the workers' milieus as part of a whole.

Country people who are swallowed up by big industrial concerns lose their traditional Catholic practices. Do they lose their faith at the same time, or don't they have any to start with? Country towns which have lost their isolation with the expansion of traffic also seem to lose their faith under the influence of the outside world.

Is this apostasy, or this weakening of faith, a result of contact with other ideologies and different moral standards which prove stronger than the existing ones? And has this contact penetrated the remotest corners of France by means of the press, the radio and the movies?

In the industries the Marxist ideology is dominant. Has it succeeded in robbing people of their faith and turning them into materialists and even atheists? It would seem so. The slogans of Communism and Socialist propaganda have become common property among the workers, undermining their confidence in the Church.

In the big cities there is materialism and the cult of pleasure, liberalism, a Voltairean skepticism and cynicism about God and religion, loose morality and an existentialist agnosticism and atheism. Have the cities infected the country? It appears so.

And if all this is true, how did it come about? Is it because industries deaden people, or because technology turns them into complacent beings susceptible to anything concrete and within their grasp, but to nothing else?

Is it because opportunities for sensual pleasures have come within reach of everybody, so that their moral resistance has crumbled and the life of the spirit has given way to the life of the moment?

Has the life of the moment become so absorbing that eternal life has been pushed into the background? Appearances indicate that it has.

And yet, there are symptoms which lead one to believe that under the surface there lie deeper sociological, psychological and ideological factors which also play a part. These are the elements of tradition. France has always been Catholic, and therefore the people want to remain Catholic. But, according to some, this Catholicism is empty. It belies what seems to be actual fact. It is something like a stubborn atavism. That may be so, but the nature of this atavism should not be too readily assumed.

In my contacts with people I have learned that their religious feelings are not solely determined by the outside, but also, and in a stronger and deeper way, by their own lives, which have in turn been shaped by centuries of Christianity. The people as a whole may dispense with all religious practices, but they will not have succeeded in becoming pure pagans. Only individuals have succeeded in this, and even in such cases I have met enough of those to know that their paganism or atheism against the background of a Christian Europe and a Christian interpretation of life is problematical, for much of Christianity has become an unconscious possession.

Is there no question, then, of dechristianization? There is and there is not.

Adherence to the Church as an organization and the practice of Christianity as a system are both decreasing. It seems evident that people have exchanged the effort of being Christians for an easy life, and their faith and their moral standards have been reduced to nothing, or almost nothing.

Organization and systematization are inherent in Christianity insofar as it is lived in community. But primary in the community is the individual. In the last analysis man faces his existence alone, and he stands alone before Christ. The Christian system is something which grew out of the living faith of individuals. Over the centuries it has reached the proportions of a monumental edifice, embellished until it has become a showpiece, a cultural monument which people come to see and admire, but in which they no longer feel at home.

The nature of human existence is always the same; man is always put on earth by God in a state of pilgrimage towards Himself. But this eternal man has, so to speak, a face of his own in every decade. As a person he is unique; he develops his personality in relation to the ever-changing world around him. The same is true of man as a Christian. The Christian outlook on life is always the same and yet ever new, but the systematization of it spans centuries. In this system there are elements which are as enduring as Christianity itself, such as the preaching of the truth and the sacramental sharing in the life of Christ. But there is also much which in different ages is felt as excess growth which chokes out life itself. In this case people struggle free of it. This struggle may appear to be a struggle against Christianity itself—especially when it includes an alienation from the authority of the Church and from the sacraments. The reaction can go too far either in the love of comfort or in the direction of fanaticism. In this respect one could really speak of a dechristianization, which is made more complete by a great ignorance of religious matters. But that still doesn't mean that the faith in God, in Christ, and in the Church as mediator in the great moments of life is lost, too. The reaction may yet be based on Christian grounds; so that the reaction which drives people too far may at the same time save them from a complete alienation from Christianity. Because they act in good faith, their error is excusable to a large extent.

In a similar way the alienation from systematized Christianity may contain important positive values. It may indicate the need for a Christianity that can be experienced personally, from within. Indifference may be an unconscious form of revolution. And a revolution is never only negative. It carries the desire for positive values within itself. This may be an unconscious return to the primary values of Christianity and of human life, from which Christianity as a system and human society as a cultural entity took their origin. One can arrive at the paradox that within the dechristianization a rebirth of Christianity may be taking place.

Only with this necessary reservation is an alienation from systematized Christianity to be interpreted as an alienation from Christianity as such. It is not without reason that the word "systematized" sounds like a kind of profanation when it is applied to Christianity. The idea of a system presupposes a human effort, a more or less artificial uniting of forces to achieve an end. Yet a system is unavoidable wherever human weakness and human society are involved. A certain understanding of reality and a certain amount of humility are necessary to submit to such systematization, even though Christianity itself is more than that. An alienation from the system can bring with it a surrender to one's own weakness. That is the vulnerable side of what can, at times, appear as a possibly encouraging re-evaluation of the primary values of Christianity and human life.

This hypothetical explanation is borne out, I feel, once one actually moves among the people. Not only can one find positive expressions of religious feeling, but in people's negative resistance and indifference to prevailing religious practices one can discover what they would like religion to be. But since their desires are not intellectually or theologically formulated and since they are hardly even conscious of them, their religious attitude appears to be entirely negative.

One should not, then, take their statements as intellectually accurate. Their *bon Dieu* is still the God of Christianity. They don't know any other.

They don't want anything to do with the Church. But the Church doesn't always mean the same thing to them, either. They don't like the French government for that matter, or that whole clique of politicians and capitalists, as they put it. But that doesn't mean that they don't want to be Frenchmen any more or have the birth of their children registered. In spite of all their criticism they take it for granted that they belong to the French nation. In the same way many of them take the Church for granted. They belong to the Church because they belong to God.

The workers' world really still belongs to the Church as a community of souls delivered by Christ. In this respect I gladly endorse the special Christian qualities with which Simon Ligier credits the workers' world in his *Essai de Psychologie Pastorale:* "Active involvement in the world; concern for dignity, liberty and justice; a sense of the autonomy of daily work; detachment from wealth and at the same time from absolute poverty; simplicity of behavior; suppression of pastoral paternalism; a substitution of authenticity for deviations like moralism, formalism or ritualism; a blossoming of hope and of a healthy eschatology." And all these qualities are based on Christianity.

Christianity is a fulfillment of man in this world, especially since the guiding impulse of his life must be love. But because the workers have become alienated from formal Christianity, they have also become alienated from the guidance of the Church and have gone back to a natural life. Nevertheless this life retains an elementary Christian orientation, and in spite of all its faults it is therefore essentially different from a purely pagan existence. What should be done is to develop their basic attitude, to strengthen and sanctify their lives with the grace of Christ.

Thus, people may be fascinated by the story of the Gospel on their own level, but it may remain a fairy tale to them, too beautiful to be realized. In that case it should be made clear to them

how the Gospel gives the answer to the basic problems of their
own existence. They should be made aware of that existence.
They are so familiar with it that it has lost meaning for them
unless they are forcefully reminded of it. Ask them how they
came to exist, and why they exist. Confront them with their long-
ing for happiness, which is the driving force in their lives and
much stronger than the misery they live in every day. Show them
how meaningless everything becomes when there is nothing but
life on this earth, and how this meaninglessness springs from the
very fact that man is not destined for this earth. Talk to them
about the nature of love, how it is related to happiness and how
it pervades man's whole existence. Show them how earthly love
always seeks the "other thing," something completely perfect;
how we depend on this "other thing," how it is the source of all
earthly joy and at the same time surpasses it entirely. How we
are destined to the complete enjoyment of this "other thing."
How, in spite of this predestination, we are unable to reach it
ourselves. How God has come to meet the conditions of man's
existence with His Revelation. How He once wished to meet man
in a unique way in Christ. How faith and hope are supported by
love. And how God's word and Christ's grace continue in the
Church. Then it will become clear to them that the shortcomings
of the Church's organization do not affect its essence. Then they
will stake themselves personally on Christianity. Then it will become reality for them instead of a fairy tale, in spite of their own
faults and those of others. Then it will be possible to bridge the
psychological gap between the workers and existing Christian
communities. Then they will know they are linked to all people
on the basis of the nature of their existence and of the Revelation,
no matter how strangely some of them may behave.

A community of like-minded people is very important, but it is
not true that a man can be a Christian solely by virtue of this
community. I can't honestly see why one should first approach the
community and only then the individual. This seems to violate
the nature of society. Christianity doesn't stir the human psyche

only when it is part of a community. It reaches far deeper, into the innermost life of the individual.

To state that the greater part of the mass cannot be led to a personal conviction would mean that most people are created primarily as herd animals and only secondarily as individuals. I don't want to deny the importance of a community for the average man, but for me this remains secondary, and I think this should be kept in mind where apostolic activity is concerned. It is not only a question of educating people to Christian practice: they must realize its meaning.

26

I HAD been told to go and see Abbé Michonneau, the parish priest of Colombes on the outskirts of Paris. I was as yet unacquainted with his writings when I went to his parish one Sunday morning. At the end of the subway line I took a bus. I passed busy Sunday markets and finally arrived at the church. People were singing inside. A Mass seemed to be in progress. I went in and tried to push the door open, but it was very hard, for people were standing against it on the inside. I finally managed to get in, but was immediately squeezed against the door myself. The church was filled to overflowing, there wasn't room for another man. I couldn't see the altar for all the people. They were in the aisles, in the corners, they were everywhere. The singing had stopped, and now there was dead silence, broken now and then by the French prayer of a priest. What could be the reason it was so crowded? People began singing again, and once in a while crossed them-

selves in unison. I couldn't get over it. Were the suburbs of Paris
not entirely dechristianized, by some chance? Or was it a special
memorial service of some kind? When the Mass was over I was
shoved helplessly outside.

"What's going on that it's so crowded?" I inquired.

"It's just Sunday, that's all."

"Yes, but is every Sunday like this?"

"Yes, the church is too small, you see. Much too small. They
have five Masses in the morning and still we can hardly get in."

"Are the other Masses so crowded, too?"

"Oh yes, the church is too small, you see."

The church was indeed not very large, but I estimated there
must have been a thousand people in it.

Some young clergymen stood talking among the people, and
also one older one. That must be Abbé Michonneau, I imagined.
In an unguarded moment I managed to get hold of him. His face
looked drawn and there were lines around his mouth and eyes.
He told me in a few words that the revival of his parish dated
from only a few years back. The neighboring parish was beginning to flourish, too. Otherwise the suburbs were still doing
poorly.

"But what is possible here, must be possible somewhere else?"

"Well . . . ."

He invited me to come by later in the week. But I didn't have
time that week, and was to discover the secret of Colombes later
in his writings.

I also met with Abbé D., the head of Catholic Action. He was
inclined to accept my diagnosis of the religious situation in
France.

"I believe France has passed its lowest point," I remarked.

"Maybe, but we shouldn't be too optimistic. As long as the
situation is seen somberly, efforts will be made. It's dangerous to
spread the notion that things aren't so bad. But we can be grateful
to God that a certain change is noticeable. A study of the kind
you're making is really very necessary. But we don't have the

people for it. One has to be very strong to be able to work incognito. It's risky."

In the rue de Babylone I stayed in a house where transient
priests of all nationalities stayed in preference to hotels. There
was a constant turnover. They took no notice of my "civilian
dress." No one asked the reason; everyone seemed to accept it
as the most natural thing in the world.

I went back to Metz in a hurry to meet a priest who had lived
for years as a worker. He, too, agreed with me. The workers' respect for Christ was touching. They were no pagans. His contact
with the workers had left a deep impression on him. He asked to
see my notes and promised to send me his.

Meanwhile I was getting tired of running around. But Gérard
was inexorable. He took me to see several other people and I was
exhausted by the time I left Metz.

My audience with Msgr. Ancel was at nine o'clock in the evening. He lived almost more simply than an ordinary priest. He
listened to me and gave me an autographed copy of *Notes doc-
trinales sur la Promotion ouvrière* of the Theological Committee
of Lyons. He was friendly and much interested, and his only
criticism of my position was that it came as no surprise to him
that the workers were open to religious influences on personal
contact.

"But a worker is also a part of the mass, and as such he is under
the influence of materialistic and Marxist doctrines. For years I
have watched the technique of the Communists, who have a
training school in our diocese. But every time I think *I* have the
people, they give me the slip. They have the masses, we don't.
Can you tell me of any mass psychology that takes the religious
as well as the secular feelings of the people into account? I don't
know a single one. A man in the mass and a man as an individual
are two different things. He is religious and secular at the same

time. And how can we reach the mass? The mass is not the sum of the individuals in it."

I was so accustomed to walking around in "civilian" clothes, that I forgot I was wearing a cassock this time. I caught myself whistling as I crossed a square and was suddenly shocked. I couldn't do that in clerical garb. Fortunately no one seemed to have noticed, and I stopped myself in time.

Early the next morning I took a train for Modena, across the French Alps. I traveled third-class. As I was walking along the corridor to get some exercise, a priest emerged from another compartment. It was Msgr. Ancel. He, too, was traveling third-class. He had taken off his bishop's ring for the occasion. We were surprised to be meeting again like this in a train corridor. He got out at the next stop.

The mountains and the entire landscape were covered by heavy snow. The sunlight was so blinding that it was impossible to look outside for long.

In Rome I was met by the friend who had made it possible for me to develop in my chosen direction. He must have been worried at times how I would make out, for he carried my suitcases as if he felt sorry for me. We drank an espresso and this marked the beginning of a new period. In Rome I felt at home. The Eternal City hadn't affected me as much the first time as it did now. As I gazed at the squares and streets with their brilliant illumination and their unending flow of traffic, I felt I was on familiar ground.